PagePlus X2 User Guide

How to Contact Us

Our main office (UK, Europe):

The Software Centre
PO Box 2000, Nottingham,
NG11 7GW, UK

Main:	(0115) 914 2000
Registration (UK only):	(0800) 376 1989
Sales (UK only):	(0800) 376 7070
Technical Support (UK only):	(0845) 345 6770
Customer Service (UK only):	(0845) 345 6770
Customer Service/	(0115) 914 9090
Tech. Support (International):	
General Fax:	(0115) 914 2020
Technical Support email:	**support@serif.co.uk**

American office (USA, Canada):

The Software Center
13 Columbia Drive, Suite 5,
Amherst NH 03031, USA

Main:	(603) 889-8650
Registration:	(800) 794-6876
Sales:	(800) 55-SERIF or 557-3743
Technical Support:	(603) 886-6642
Customer Service:	(800) 489-6720
General Fax:	(603) 889-1127
Technical Support email:	**support@serif.com**

Online

Visit us on the Web at:	**http://www.serif.com/**
Serif forums:	**http://www.serif.com/forums.asp**

International

Please contact your local distributor/dealer. For further details please contact us at one of
our phone numbers above.

Comments or other feedback

We want to hear from you! Please email **feedback@serif.com** with your ideas and
comments!

In memory of Robert Evans, dedicated member of the Serif Development team,
and Dave Paddock, beta tester and long time supporter of Serif Products.

Contents

Contents

6. Working with Images, Lines, and Shapes 133

Contents

Contents

Welcome

Welcome to PagePlus X2!

PagePlus X2

Welcome to **PagePlus**: the latest in the best-selling, award-winning PagePlus line—still the easiest way to get superior publishing results, whether on your desktop or via professional printing.

If you've used PagePlus in the past, you know that **PagePlus does it all**—from glossy corporate marketing materials to "fun stuff" like party invites, brochures, business stationery (cards, letterheads, compliment slips, and envelopes), invoices, flyers, forms, newsletters, notices, handouts, event programs, posters, price lists, reports, announcements, greeting cards, and much more. And of course, Web sites, too! With your PC, printer, and PagePlus, you can save time and money—no experience required.

What's New in PagePlus X2...

- **PDF Slideshows—be a show off!** (see p. 203)
  Share your very own slideshows. Create multi-section slide variants based on page layers, add inter-page transitions (**Blinds**, **Wipe**, **Dissolve**, amongst others), and control slide arrangement, as well as slide display duration. Add sound accompaniment, along with placed sound and movie clips, and you've got a cool desktop presentation with no fuss.

- **Work that Media!** (see p. 140)
  No more repetitive photo importing! Keep photo content to hand in the new **Media Bar**. Create your own photo-rich documents or **Photo Albums** from design templates, then **AutoFlow** photos (or drag and drop) from the Media Bar into picture frames! Searching of metadata (XMP, IPTC, and EXIF) offers powerful photo retrieval—even add your own keywords to photos (XMP metadata).

- **Text and style formatting!**
  Ctrl-select multiple words or paragraphs (frame or artistic text alike) to apply common formatting (p. 75). Apply **multi-level bullet and numbering schemas** (p. 100) to your paragraphs, even to your Text Styles! Feel like changing the same text style used in your PagePlus document for another?—all possible from the new **Text Styles tab** (p. 90), which sports **in-situ** style previews with **bulk text style replacement**!

- **Font preview, search and replacement** (see p. 85)
  View your currently installed font set in the **Fonts tab**, including those most recently assigned to text. The tab also hosts a quick search feature to filter fonts by name, attribute, or type. Hover over a listed font for an **in-situ** font preview of your selected text—simply click to apply the new font if you like it! Easily **swap** all instances of a common font for another font in one fell swoop!

- **Desktop and Commercial Design Templates** (see p. 20)
  Fancy a quick route to produce stunning designs for home or business use? Adopt one of an impressive collection of **Design Templates** ranging from **Photo Albums**, **Calendars**, **Publications**, **Greeting Cards**, or **CD/DVD Labels** (Avery compatible) to business-related **Flyers**, **Forms**, **Stationery**, **email** and **web sites** templates. Using Photo Album multi-page templates?—base a new page on an existing template page or optionally use template page variants.

- **Connectors** (see p. 167)
  Benefit from connectors when drawing dynamic flow diagrams, family trees, organization charts—connectors will link your boxes, circles, or other shapes together, with links being maintained during any object repositioning. The **Connector Tool** and **Elbow Connector Tool** will route between objects with ease!

- **How To tab—documentation at your fingertips** (see PagePlus help)
  The tab offers a wide range of task-based How To topics most commonly asked for by PagePlus users, all accessible via sample page layouts with clickable page elements—use as an always available handy reference! Tips, frequently asked questions, tricks, and shortcuts also complement the tab.

- **Instant3D with on-screen transforms** (see p. 163)
  Transform 3D objects **in-situ** with 3D editing from context toolbar. Apply awesome multi-coloured **lighting effects** (with directional control), along with custom **bevel** and **lathe** effect profiles to create your very own unique contours. **Hardware-accelerated rendering** boosts redraw performance (hardware dependent).

- **Instant Shadows!** (see p. 158)
  The new **Shadow Tool** makes light work of adding shadows to pictures and artistic text.. in fact any PagePlus object. Basic or skewed shadows can be adjusted on the page with control handles—modify shadow colour, intensity, and blur, or change position, angle and shear.

- **Send as HTML** (see p. 207)
  Send your page design via email in HTML format, safe in the knowledge that pictures and hyperlinks are maintained. Take advantage of ready-made email design templates—holiday, blog, birthday, or business—to make someone's day.

- **Picture frames** (see p. 138)
  Pick from a selection of picture frames—choose a shaped **heart**, **star**, **triangle**, or **flower** preset, amongst many others. Drag pictures from the new Media Bar or **Replace Picture** with full control over picture sizing and alignment within the frame. Interested in frame borders? Simply select from the Gallery tab.

- **Year update for Calendars plus inline events!** (see p. 118)
  Update your calendar's year and add named personal events, plus country- or region-specific public holidays, all with powerful event control (**Calendar Event Manager**).

- **Enhanced tables** (see p. 110)
  Distribute or **autofit** selected rows, columns, or your entire table—even set absolute row/column sizes! **Sort** single- or multi-column/row contents. Now benefit from **resizing** of table columns without affecting table width.

- **Layout aids** (see p. 40)
  Take advantage of labour-saving **"sticky" guides**, a great way of moving (in bulk) all objects snapped to your ruler guides—move the guide and objects will follow!

- **Tab controls and your workspace** (see PagePlus help)
  PagePlus now features auto show/hide tab controls, with supporting slide, fade, or roll animation effects—you can promote tabs into view while hiding rarely used tabs. Favourite user-defined workspace profiles can be loaded from the Startup Wizard (or use a preset workspace profile).

- **Enhanced PDF export/import** (see p. 201)
  Play **sound** and **movie clips** in exported PDFs—great for the new PDF slideshow feature! Export PDFs with native alpha-channel transparency support. Unicode text is exported without conversion to curves, while greyscale/monochrome image export is enhanced. Preserve font appearance from **imported PDFs** with PagePlus's PDF embedded font support—avoiding font substitution issues!

- **Enhanced FTP upload (Web Publishing mode)** (see p. 229)
  New FTP features include uploading your PagePlus project to safeguard against loss. Manually control which files to upload during more versatile incremental updates. Fancy a fresh start? Now delete the entire site in one operation.

- **Fully Vista Compatible!** (see PagePlus help)
  Using Microsoft's new Operating System? Remember to visit the **Text Search** feature to display text from all open PagePlus documents at the same time. View resizable large-format **thumbnail previews** of any PagePlus publications in the Vista Explorer.

- **..and some very useful additions you've been asking for!**
  Improved page **auto-panning** and **Text on a Path** operations. Use **Select All** in the **Find & Replace** feature to view all matching text instances. Express **text leading** as a percentage of point size. Use optical justification to produce a hanging indent on your frame text's punctuation—great for tidy margin edges. Create shaped text frames by typing directly onto any shape—great for diagrams and illustrations! **Resize a cropped picture** within its crop area. Preview publications in **Trimmed Page Mode** and continue designing—all at the same time! The re-designed **Transform tab** supports origin control for unlimited resizing, stretching and rotating. **Sort paragraph lists** either alphabetically or numerically. Line styles now let you **scale line ends** (e.g., arrows) and control line end placement. For professional printing, import and manipulate CMYK .JPG files and make use of Adobe-based ICC colour profiles shipped with PagePlus.

Existing Features

DTP revolutionized the graphics arts industry, and PagePlus revolutionized the DTP market—with high-impact design available to everyone. Features such as...

- **Versatile Setup with Auto-Imposition**
  Just click to specify layouts for small (business cards and labels), folded (booklets and greetings cards), and large publications (banners and posters)!

- **Mail Merge**
  With Mail and Photo Merge, read data from just about any source: tables from HTML Web pages, database files, even live ODBC servers!

- **Superior Text Entry and Unicode Support**
  Import, paste, export in **Unicode** format... design with a foreign-language or special fonts and characters.

- **Augmented Text Editing Capabilities, Convenience**
  Instantly fill new frames with "dummy" text for pre-final layout design, or click the **AutoFlow** button anytime to generate new frames and pages for longer stories. Use drag-and-drop editing in WritePlus. Clear formatting (revert to plain style) with a single keystroke. Enhanced **Find and Replace** features "wild card" capability using regular expressions.

- **Clipboard and Object Controls**
  The **Paste in Place** command lets you manipulate objects more efficiently. Between objects, align and snap to object centres... use **Paste Format** to transfer any or all attributes. On single objects, apply a **border** to selected edges... include or exclude specific filter effects.

- **Swap Styles with a Single Click**
  Select any object (including text) and choose from a gallery of ready-made styles that **combine a host of attributes** such as 3D filter effects, glows, shadows, textures, and materials. Customize the preset styles or create your own!

- **Packed Gallery of Designs**
  Use the **Gallery tab** to store your favourite designs for use in any publication! Alternatively, use the categorized galleries to select from an impressive collection of pre-defined designs—simply drag to the page.

- **Frame Text and Artistic Text**

  Compose traditional **text in frames**, rotate or reshape frames and still edit their text. And **artistic text** lets you click and type anywhere on the page, format with the customary tools, then apply colourful lines and fills directly at the character level. Scale it, rotate it, flip it... **flow it along a path**!

- **Text Composition Tools**

  PagePlus includes word count, search and replace, spell-checking, thesaurus, and proof reader. AutoCorrect and AutoSpell proofing options are at hand.

- **Multilingual Support**

  Create **multiple language** documents (14 dictionaries are provided including German, French, Spanish, and Italian) in PagePlus. You can mark words, paragraphs or whole stories with a language and PagePlus will automatically check the spelling for you in that language. Mix and match multiple languages in one document if you want.

- **Automatic Font Substitution**

  PANOSE©-matching **substitution of fonts** on import resolves possible missing font issues with the option of manually re-mapping fonts at a later date.

- **Professional Layout Tools**

  Multipage view lets you **see an array of pages**, not just one at a time. Intelligent text fitting. Movable rulers and guides. Precision placement, rotation, and **text wrap**. Flip, crop, watermark, and recolour graphics. Text formatting with bullets, lists, kerning, hyphenation, drop caps, smart quotes, and named styles. Multiple master pages with **as many separate background templates as you need**. Each page can have multiple layers—so you can assign elements to different layers for modular design. Facing pages display, and much more!

- **QuickShapes**

  As with other Serif solutions, **QuickShapes** provide intelligent clipart for your publication.

- **Powerful Drawing Options**

  Sketch **freehand lines and curves**, extend existing lines with ease... simply "connect the dots" to **trace around curved objects** and pictures. Use the Curve context toolbar to **fine-tune contours or edit Bézier nodes**. Sketch using **calligraphic lines**, add rounded corners (caps), vary the join style of connected lines. Connect end points to create any shape you like! Apply **line styles** to all kinds of shapes—even add line endings like arrowheads and diamonds. Customize line and fill, apply transparency, even freely edit the outline. Automatic anti-aliasing of lines, text, and polygons results in superb visuals, both on-screen and on the printed page.

- **Powerful Shape Conversion Options**

  The **Convert to Curves** command gives you node-and-segment control over all objects, including QuickShapes. **Convert to Shaped Frame** lets you create a text container out of any shape you can draw! And with **Crop to Shape** you can use any top shape's outline to trim another below. And try **combining curves** to create "holes" for mask or stencil effects.

- **A New Slant with Enveloping**

  Apply a customizable **mesh warp envelope** to any object to add perspective, slant, bulge, and more.

- **Control Colour in an instant**

  Use the Colour tab to change fill, line, or text colour on any selected object(s) with one click. Automatically store you currently used publication's colours in the Swatches tab's Publication palette (great for future use). Alternatively, choose from a vast array of preset fills (solid, gradient, or bitmap) in the Swatches tab's palettes—different standard, custom, or themed palettes can be loaded. View, edit or delete colours you have been using in any palette, or add your own!

- **Intelligent Colour Schemes**

  Choose from dozens of preset **colour schemes** to change the overall appearance of your publications with a single click. You can customize the scheme colours, create brand new schemes, and apply any scheme to a "from-scratch" publication.

- **Transparency Effects**

  Both **solid and variable transparency** let you add new depth to your print and Web creations. Apply transparency directly from the Transparency tab, then edit nodes and opacity with the interactive tool. Get set for fun with Photo Edge Effects and a host of other Bitmap transparencies!

- **Astounding 3D Lighting and Surface Effects**
  Beyond **shadow, glow, bevel, and emboss**, advanced algorithms **bring flat shapes to life**! Choose one or more effects, then vary surface and source light properties. Start with a pattern or a function, adjust parameters for incredible surface contours, textures, fills— realistic-looking wood, water, skin, marble and much more. The **Feathering** filter effect adds a soft or blurry edge to any object. **Instant 3D** adds realistic depth to ordinary objects and text. Use one master control panel to vary extrusion, rotation, bevel, lighting, texture, and more.

- **Versatile Text Shape and Flow**
  You can **rotate or reshape text frames** and still edit their text. Enhanced **text wrap options** and separate crop and wrap outlines mean you have greater control over where text flows and how it appears.

- **Impressive Graphics Handling**
  Convert to Picture allows instant, in-place format changes! TIFFs retain CMYK colour data for full colour separation. Linked images are easy to maintain... and each export filter remembers its own settings. For more accurate results with professional printing, you can **switch in a flash** to a CMYK palette.

- **Picture Import and Adjustments**
  Import images inline as part of frame text flow, and create your own 32-bit anti-aliased TIFFs and PNGs. Benefit from "on-board" image adjustments for making quick fixes to imported images—eliminate the dreaded red eye effect on subjects in your photos with the new **Red Eye Tool**. Alternatively, pick from **Auto Levels, Auto Contrast, Brightness/Contrast, Channel Mixer, Colour Balance, Curves**, and many more. Commonly used special effects such as **Diffuse Glow, Dust and Scratch Remover, Shadows/Highlights**, and various blurs make up the set of adjustments, which can be applied in combination. For advanced photo manipulation use the **Edit in PhotoPlus** option from within PagePlus to edit and save images and PhotoPlus files with impressive synergy. Use the Picture context toolbar to adjust size and resolution, apply colouration or transparency. **Add instant borders** to your imported pictures.

- **Photo Optimizer**
  If your publication includes colour or greyscale photographs, use the Photo Optimizer to get the best results for each photo on your particular printer. Pick the best result from the thumbnail sheet—and PagePlus remembers the optimum settings for that image!

- **Table Tool with Editable Calendars**
  Create and edit tables, with no need for a separate utility. Choose from a range of preset formats or design your own by customizing lines, cells, rows, and columns. Use the convenient Table context toolbar to enter text, apply **preset or custom number formatting**, and choose from a wide range of **functions** for spreadsheet calculations.. even **display data from databases directly**. Powerful text manipulation features... and calendars are table-based for enhanced functionality!

- **Index, Table of Contents, and Calendar Wizards**
  Compile a professional **index** complete with headings, subheadings, and page references... especially useful for longer publications! Automatically collect newsletter headlines (or any styled text you specify) into a **table of contents** list! For calendars, choose from a wide variety of sizes and design options, then just click and drag to fit your **calendar** to a column or a whole page!

- **Books Have Arrived on Your Desktop!**
  Treat separate PagePlus publication files as chapters and use the **BookPlus** utility to link them into a book!

- **Versatile Desktop Printing and Mail Merge**
  Impressive results on your dot-matrix, ink-jet, or laser printer in black and white or full colour. Print your current publication multiple times, **merging data** from any character-delimited address list file.

- **PDF Output for Pro Printing or Electronic Distribution...**
  Press-ready PDF/X file includes all fonts and colour information for spot or process colour... and PDF ensures a secure, cross-platform electronic alternative to paper-based publishing, with Bookmarks, PageHints, and file protection! Add Web-style **hyperlinks** directly... automatically generate a **bookmark list** (table of contents) using styled text markup. Export with optional PDF streaming for faster Web-based downloads!

- **Import PDF**
  Import PDF documents as new PagePlus publications or insert a PDF document's contents into existing publications. Either way, PDF contents can be easily edited within PagePlus—the text and paragraph formatting of the original PDF document is maintained.

- **PDF Forms for electronic form completion**
  Create and publish PDF forms such as membership forms, invoices, and surveys with an easy to follow **Form Submit Wizard**. Form recipients can fill-out a circulated electronic form and print, save and/or submit their form data across the Web or to your email address using "**Serif Web Resources**", which provides web-to-email service for registered Serif customers. Generated forms can be certified by author and signed by form recipients.

- **Web Publishing Mode**
  Create your own Web site using web-based Design Templates or convert an existing PagePlus publication to a Web site! The Layout Checker helps you fine-tune your design. Preview your site in a Web browser and publish it to a local folder or a remote server. Use FTP-based **maintenance mode** with familiar Explorer-style controls.

- **Sharing your publication**
  Send your PagePlus project via email to share or collaborate with friend, family and colleagues!

- **Total Ease-of-Use**
  Context toolbars are available whose tools and options dynamically change according to the currently selected object in your publication. This ensures that the most common options are always at your fingertips. Toolbars can be customized while Studio tabs can be docked, grouped, resized, or hidden to increase your workspace area; save your preferred workspace settings to file for instant recall whenever you wish. And there's more: The **Replicate tool** instantly multiplies any object into a line or grid arrangement. You can drag and drop objects from other applications, select multiple Undo and Redo actions selectable from a handy list. **Import Photoshop .PSD files** with clipped paths.

Registration, Upgrades and Support

If you see the Registration Wizard when you launch PagePlus, please take a moment to complete the registration process. Follow the simple on-screen instructions and you'll be supplied a personalized registration number in return. If you need technical support please contact us, we aim to provide fast, friendly service and knowledgeable help. There's also a wide range of support information available 24 hours a day on our website at **www.serif.com**.

Installation

System Requirements

If you need help installing Windows, or setting up peripherals, see Windows documentation and help.

Minimum:

- Pentium PC with CD-ROM/DVD-ROM drive and mouse (or other Microsoft-compatible pointing device)

- Microsoft Windows® 2000, XP, or Vista operating system

- 256MB RAM minimum

- 496MB (recommended install) free hard disk space (Program CD only)

- SVGA (800x600 resolution, 16-bit colour) display or higher.

Additional disk resources and memory are required when editing large or complex documents.

Optional:

- Windows-compatible printer

- TWAIN-compatible scanner and/or digital camera

- Stylus or other input device

- 3D Accelerated graphics card with DirectX 9 (or above) or OpenGL support

- Internet account and connection required for Web Publishing features and accessing online resources

First-time Install

To install PagePlus X2, simply insert the Program CD-ROM into your CD-ROM drive. The AutoRun feature automatically starts the Setup process and all you need to do is answer the on-screen questions. If the AutoRun does not start the install, use the manual install instructions below.

If you've also obtained the PagePlus X2 Resource CD, install it now following the same procedure you used for the Program CD.

Manual Install/Re-install

To re-install the software or to change any part of the installation at a later date, select **Control Panel** from the Windows **Start** menu (via the Settings item for pre-XP systems) and then double-click the **Add/Remove Programs** icon. Make sure the correct CD-ROM is inserted into your CD-ROM drive, choose **Serif PagePlus X2**, and click the **Install…** button. You'll have the choice of removing or adding components, re-installing components, or removing all components.

Other PagePlus Resources

Resource CD-ROM

The Resource CD includes many professionally designed design templates for instantly creating brochures, business forms, calendars, stationery, notices, newsletters, Web sites, and much more. In addition, you'll find a set of illustrated tutorials for hands-on projects and a great learning experience.

Resource Guide

The Resource Guide provides a compendium of reference material to help any user get the most out of PagePlus. At-a-glance, full colour previews of PagePlus design templates, Image Galleries, and more... plus convenient access to a range of tutorials at all levels. The Guide is something to keep handy and return to time and time again.

About this User Guide

This User Guide focuses on information essential to the design, publishing and printing of your PagePlus publication. As a feature-rich product, PagePlus supports many more features which can't all be included in this User Guide. To assist, the following table lists some other books and topics exclusively available within the PagePlus Online Help. Scan the help's **Contents** for these books and topics for more information!

Book Name	Topics covered in book...
How to Start, Save and Close Publications	Saving your own templates
How to Work with Pages	Working with layers
How to Work with Objects	Converting an object to a picture Exporting as a picture
How to Format Characters and Paragraphs	Adjusting letter spacing and kerning
How to Use Special Character Options	Using hyphenation
How to Use Advanced Document Features	Exporting story text Merging photos and other pictures Merging into a repeating layout
How to Work with Lines and Shapes	Understanding blend modes
How to Import Images and Objects	Importing PhotoCD images Importing TWAIN images
How to Apply Image Adjustments	Applying Adjustments
How to Work with Colour, Fills, and Transparency	Changing or copying image colours Colour matching with PANTONE® colours Managing screen and output colours
How to Prepare a Publication for the Web	Adding rollovers Setting Web picture display options Adding HTML Adding search engine descriptors Optimizing your Web site

Getting Started

Getting Started

Startup Wizard

Once PagePlus has been installed, you're ready to start. Setup adds a **Serif PagePlus X2** item to the **(All) Programs** submenu of the Windows Start menu.

- Use the Windows **Start** button to start PagePlus (or if PagePlus is already running, choose **New>New from Startup Wizard...** from the File menu) to display the Startup Wizard (menu screen).

The Startup Wizard presents the following choices:

- **Use a design template**, to create an instant document from a pre-designed template

- **Start from scratch**, to open a blank page to work on

- **Open a publication**, to edit a saved PagePlus file

- **View tutorials**, to see step-by-step PagePlus projects

- **Choose a workspace**, to adopt the default workspace profile <**Default Profile**>, the last used profile <**Current Profile**>, a range of profile presets, or a workspace profile you have previously saved. Each workspace profile stores Studio tab positions, tab sizes, and displayed and hidden tab options.

Creating a publication from a design template

It's so much easier creating publications with a little bit of help—PagePlus comes complete with a whole range of categorized design templates (Photo Albums, Greeting Cards, CD/DVD labels, etc.) which will speed you through the creation of all kinds of publications for desktop or commercial printing—even your own Web site! PagePlus ships with a selection of design templates, and many more are available on the *PagePlus X2 Resource* CD.

Templates help ensure continuity between your publications by preserving starting setups for such elements as page layout, contents, styles, and colour palettes.

Design templates from the Photo Album categories provide additional alternative single page layouts which can be adopted when adding more pages to your document. (See **Adding, Removing and Rearranging Pages** on p. 34).

To create a publication from a design template:

1. Open PagePlus, or choose **New...** from the File menu and select **New from Startup Wizard...**.

2. Click **use a design template**.

3. In the **Templates** list on the left, select a publication category and then examine the samples on the right. Click the sample that is the closest match to the document you want to create and then click **Open**.

This method is the only way to access design templates. If you've switched the Startup Wizard off (and don't see it when you start up or choose **File>New...**), you can switch it on again: On the **Tools** menu, choose **Options**. Then, on the **General** page, select **Use startup wizard**.

You can save any PagePlus document as a template (*.PPX) file to be used as a basis for other publications. When opening a saved template file, PagePlus automatically opens an untitled copy, leaving the original template intact. See PagePlus help for more details.

Starting a new publication from scratch

Although **design templates** can simplify your design choices, you can just as easily start out from scratch with a new, blank publication.

To start a new publication of a certain type:

1. Open PagePlus, or choose **New...** from the File menu and select **New from Startup Wizard...**.

2. Click **start from scratch**.

3. In the **Templates** list on the left, select a publication type and then examine the samples on the right. Click the sample that is the closest match to the document you want to create (you can select from the given publication types or define a custom publication by clicking **Custom Page Setup...**).

4. Click **Open** to open a new publication with a blank page.

> If you click **Cancel** (or press **Escape**) from the Startup Wizard, PagePlus opens a blank document using default page properties.

To start a new default publication:

- Click the ⬜ **New Publication** button on the Standard toolbar (only available if the Startup Wizard is turned off).

To turn off the Startup Wizard:

- Choose **Options** from the Tools menu and uncheck **Use Startup Wizard** from the General menu item.

Opening an existing publication

You can open an existing PagePlus publication either from the Startup Wizard or from within PagePlus.

To open an existing publication from the Startup Wizard:

1. Select the **open a publication** option. In the Documents pane of the **Open Saved Work** dialog, you'll see either your computer's folder structure for navigation to your publications (Folders tab) or a list of most recently used PagePlus publications (History tab). Preview thumbnails or publication details can be shown in the adjacent pane depending on your current view.

2. Click a file name or sample, then click **Open**.

To open an existing publication from within PagePlus:

1. Click the 🖆 **Open** button on the Standard toolbar.

2. In the Open dialog, select the folder and file name and click the **Open** button.

To revert to the saved version of an open publication:

*   Choose **Revert** from the File menu.

Importing PagePlus documents

It is possible to import any PagePlus document into your currently loaded PagePlus document, typically to reuse content. The character formatting, layout and images used in the original document are maintained to honour the look and feel of the original content. Any font used in the original file but not present on your computer will be **substituted** with another replacement font.

The pages of the imported PagePlus document can be inserted into the currently open publication before or after a currently selected page, or can replace the current page.

To insert a PagePlus document into an existing PagePlus document:

1. Open your existing PagePlus document.

2. Select a page from the Pages tab (remember to double-click the page to select) or from the navigation buttons on the Hintline toolbar.

3. Choose **Insert>PagePlus File...** from the Insert menu.

4. In the Open dialog, navigate to and select the PagePlus document for insertion. Click **Open**.

5. From the **Insert PagePlus File** dialog, choose to insert the pages of the imported PDF document **Before the current page**, **On the current page**, or **After the current page**.

6. If necessary, check the options to group each new page as a single object and to resize your current publication to that of your inserted PagePlus document.

7. Click the **OK** button.

Importing PDF files

It is possible to import any PDF document created with other applications directly into PagePlus to create either a new PagePlus publication or to add to an existing publication. The character formatting, layout and images in the original PDF document are preserved to allow comprehensive editing of the document.

To honour the look and feel of an original PDF file, any font embedded in the original PDF (and which is used in imported text) is extracted from the imported PDF file and installed automatically. The document containing the imported PDF content will only make the font available if it is embedded in the project. This is true of TrueType (TTF) fonts and OpenType fonts with TTF or Type 1 outlines, but PostScript Type 1 fonts themselves are not supported.

 The embedded font can't be used for other documents or applications and will not appear in the Windows Fonts folder.

The pages of a PDF document can be inserted into a currently open publication before or after a currently selected page, or can replace the current page.

To import a PDF file to create a PagePlus publication:

1. Select **File>Open....**

2. Select the name of the file, and click Open. The PDF document is imported and will repaginate to the number of pages of the original PDF document.

3. Click **OK**.

4. Use **File>Save** to save as a PagePlus publication (*.PPP).

To insert a PDF file into an existing PagePlus publication:

1. Open your existing PagePlus publication.

2. Select a page from the Pages tab (remember to double-click the page to select) or from the navigation buttons on the Hintline toolbar.

3. Choose **Insert>PDF File...** from the Insert menu.

4. In the Open dialog, navigate to and select the PDF file for insertion. Click **Open**.

5. From the **Insert PDF File** dialog, choose to insert the pages of the imported PDF document **Before the current page**, **On the current page** or **After the current page**.

6. If necessary, check the options to group each new page as a single object and to resize your current publication to that of your inserted PDF document.

7. Click the **OK** button.

Working with more than one publication

PagePlus lets you open more than one publication at a time, and work with more than one window for a given publication. You can drag and drop objects between publication windows.

Each new publication you open appears in a separate window with its own settings.

To close the current window:

- Choose **Close** from the File menu or click the window's ⊠ **Close** button. If it's the only window open for the publication, the command closes the publication and you'll be prompted to save changes.

 You can close all open publications without exiting the main PagePlus application.

The Window menu lets you create new windows and arrange the open document windows in various ways, i.e. by cascading and tiling horizontally or vertically.

Saving your publication

To save your work:

- Click the 📄 **Save** button on the Standard toolbar.
  OR
  To save under a different name, choose **Save As...** from the File menu.

Closing PagePlus

To close the current window:

- Choose **Close** from the File menu or click the window's 🗵 **Close** button. If it's the only window open for the publication, the command closes the publication and you'll be prompted to save changes.

To close PagePlus:

- Click the program's 🗵 **Close** button at the top right of the window.
  OR
  Choose **Exit** from the File menu.

You'll be prompted to save changes to any open publications.

Updating and saving defaults

Object defaults are the stored property settings PagePlus applies to <u>newly created</u> text, graphics, and frames. When you create text in your publication, it will have default properties for font, size, colour, alignment, etc. New graphics will have default properties for line and fill colour, shade, pattern, etc. New frames will have default properties for margins, columns, etc. You can easily change the defaults for any type of object.

Default settings are always **local**—that is, any changed defaults apply to the current publication and are automatically saved with it, so they're in effect next time you open that publication. However, at any time you can use the Save Defaults command to record the current defaults as **global** settings that will be in effect for any new publication you subsequently create.

To set local defaults for a particular type of object:

1. Create a single sample object and fine-tune its properties as desired—or use an existing object that already has the right properties. (For graphics, you can use a line, shape, or rectangle; all share the same set of defaults.)

2. Select the object that's the basis for the new defaults and choose **Update Object Default** from the Format menu (or **Update Text Default** for text).
    OR
    Right-click the sample object and choose **Format>Update Object Default** (or **Text Format>Update Text Default**).

Or, for line and fill colours, including line styles:

1. With no object selected, choose the required line and/or fill colours from the Colour or Swatches tab. Use the Line tab to set a default line weight, style, and corner shape.

2. Draw your object on the page, which will automatically adopt the newly defined default colours and styles.

You can also view and change the current default text properties in the Text Style Palette.

To view and change default text properties:

1. Choose **Text Style Palette...** from the Format menu.

2. Click **Default Text**, then click **Modify...** to view current settings.

3. Use the **Attributes** button to alter character, paragraph, or other properties.

To save all current defaults as global settings:

1. Choose **Save Defaults** from the Tools menu.

2. Click **OK** to confirm that you want new publications to use the current publication's defaults.

Working with Pages

Setting up a publication

A publication's **page size** and **orientation** settings are fundamental to your layout, and are defined when the new publication is first created, either **using a design template** or as a **New Publication** choice via **File>New...** and the Startup Wizard. If the Startup Wizard is turned off, or you cancel the setup dialog, a new publication defaults to A4 (Europe) or Letter size (US). PagePlus can handle nearly unlimited page sizes. In practice, your working limit is likely to be set by the capabilities of your desktop printer.

To adjust size/orientation of the current publication (Paper Publishing mode):

1. On the File menu, choose **Page Setup....**

2. For **Regular/Booklet** publications, you can select a pre-defined paper size or enter custom values for page width and height, as well as setting the orientation (Portrait or Landscape).

3. For other publication types, you can select the publication types: Small (for example, business cards, labels, etc.), Large (banners or posters), or Folded (booklets).

4. Choose a pre-defined option from the list (use the preview) or to define a custom publication based on the selected option, click **Create Custom....**

5. Add additional custom settings if necessary.

6. Click **OK** to accept the new dimensions. The updated settings will be applied to the current publication.

To adjust size/orientation of the current publication (Web Publishing mode):

1. Choose **Page Setup...** from the File menu.

2. Set page dimensions as **Standard** for VGA monitors (recommended), **Wide** for SVGA, or **Custom**. For a custom setting, enter page dimensions in pixels.

Facing pages

In Paper Publishing mode, you can set up your publication so that the PagePlus window displays pages either singly or in pairs—as two facing pages side by side. You'll need facing pages if you're creating a publication where you need to see both the left-hand (verso) and right-hand (recto) pages, or one that employs double-page spreads where a headline or other element needs to run from the left-hand page to the right-hand page.

To set up facing pages (Paper Publishing mode):

1. In the **Page Setup** dialog, check **Facing Pages**.

2. If you plan to use background elements that span a double-page spread, select **Dual master pages**. This will let you define master pages with paired "left page" and "right page" components.

   OR

   For a facing-page layout where both left and right pages initially share the same master page, and you don't need to run background elements across the spread, clear **Dual master pages**.

Because you assign master pages to individual page layers, one page at a time, it takes two separate steps to assign a dual master page to both left and right facing pages. For details, see **Assigning master pages**.

You can assign different master pages to the left and right publication pages if necessary. For example (see below), a left-hand "body text" page might use the left-side component of one master page, while a right-hand "chapter divider" page could use the right side of a different master page.

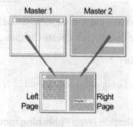

Understanding master pages

In PagePlus, single pages are the basic organizational unit, with each page built up using multiple levels and layers, and by **ordering** layout elements in a stack on each layer.

Master pages

Master pages provide a flexible way to store background elements that you'd like to appear on more than one page—for example a logo, background, header/footer, or border design.

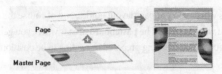

The key concept here is that a particular master page is typically **shared** by multiple pages, as illustrated below. By placing a design element on a master page and then assigning several pages to use that master page, you ensure that all the pages incorporate that element. Of course, each individual page can have its own "foreground" elements.

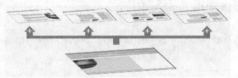

Master pages are available in every publication, but in a simple publication you may not need to use any master pages—or you may need only one master page. Facing pages and multiple master pages prove valuable with longer, more complex publications. Using the **Pages** tab or **Page Manager**, you can quickly add or delete master pages; for example, you could set up different master pages for "title" or "chapter divider" pages. For details, see **Adding, removing, and rearranging pages** on p. 34, including how to edit the design elements on a master page by switching the working view to the master page level.

Viewing pages

Most of the PagePlus display is taken up by a page or "artwork" area and a surrounding "pasteboard" area.

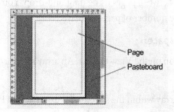

In PagePlus, the **page area** is where you put page layout guides, and of course the text, shapes, and pictures that you want to print. The **pasteboard area** is where you generally keep any text, shapes, or pictures that are being prepared or waiting to be positioned on the page area.

To move or copy an object between pages via the Pasteboard:

1. Drag the object onto the pasteboard (hold down the **Ctrl** key to copy).

2. Use the page navigation buttons on the HintLine toolbar to change pages.

3. Drag the object from the pasteboard onto the new page.

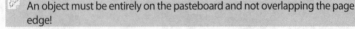

An object must be entirely on the pasteboard and not overlapping the page edge!

View controls

PagePlus makes it easy to see exactly what you're working on—from a wide view of multiple pages to a close-up view of a small region. For example, you can use the **scrollbars** at the right and bottom of the main window to move the page and pasteboard with respect to the main window. If you're using a **wheel mouse**, you can scroll vertically by rotating the wheel, or horizontally by **Shift**-rotating.

The View toolbar at the top of the screen provides the 🖐 **Pan Tool** as an alternative way of moving around, plus a number of buttons that let you zoom in and out so you can inspect and/or edit the page at different levels of detail.

You can switch between two viewing modes: **Normal** view, which displays one page at a time, and **Multi-page** view, which displays a number of pages at a time in the workspace. In either mode, the pasteboard is shared by all pages. In Multi-page view, it's especially easy to move or copy objects between pages using drag-and-drop. You can easily switch between modes and set the number of pages displayed.

To view multiple pages in the workspace:

1. Click the ▦ **Multi-page** button on the View toolbar. An array selector appears.

2. Click and drag to choose an array within the selector, for example 2x4 Pages or 3x1 Pages (as shown). To expand the number of choices, drag down and to the right. Click **Normal View** if you change your mind.

The publication appears in Multipage mode with the specified page array in view.

To switch between Normal and Multi-page view:

- Choose **Normal** or **Multi-page** from the View menu.

In either mode, you can use the ◀ **Previous Page** and ▶ **Next Page** buttons on the HintLine toolbar to step between pages. In Multi-page view, you have the additional option of scrolling from one set of pages to the next using the vertical scrollbar or the Pan Tool.

Navigating

However you choose to structure your publication, PagePlus provides a variety of ways of getting quickly to the elements you need to edit.

To go to a publication page/master page:

1. On the **Pages** tab, your publication pages appear as thumbnails in the main Pages panel (in page number order).

2. Double-click on a thumbnail in the panel—use the page numbering underneath each thumbnail for navigation. Your selected page is displayed.

For Master pages, click on the Master Pages ▶ button to expand the Master Pages panel, and double-click on a master page.

Alternatively, you can use the ▦ **Page Manager** (View tab) on the HintLine toolbar.

To go to an adjacent page/master page:

- Switch to the level (page or master page) you want to work on, as described **below**, then click the ◀ **Previous Page** or ▶ **Next Page** button on the HintLine toolbar.

To go to the first or last page/master page:

- Switch to the level (page or master page) you want to work on, as described **below**, then click the ◀ **First Page** or ▶ **Last Page** button on the HintLine toolbar.

Once you've displayed a page/master page, you can normally edit any object on it—regardless of the layer the object is on—simply by clicking the object. In order to create a new object on a particular layer, you'll first need to "activate" (switch to) that layer.

To switch to a particular layer of a page/master page:

- After displaying the page or master page, double-click the layer's name (or click to the left of the layer's entry) in the Layers tab.

The active layer becomes uppermost in the workspace, and a ▶ mark appears next to its entry in the Layers tab.

The master page level

In order to add or edit master page elements, you first need to switch from the regular page level of the publication to the master page level.

To switch between page and master page levels:

- Double-click a thumbnail on the Pages tab to go directly to that page or master page (lower and upper pages, respectively).
  OR

- Click once on the page name or number on the Hintline.

Adding, removing, and rearranging pages

Use the **Pages** tab to quickly rearrange pages using drag-and-drop, and add or delete standard pages or **master pages**. The tab displays master pages in the upper (collapsible) **Master Pages** panel and standard publication pages in the lower **Pages** panel.

The **Page Manager**, accessible from the ▣ **Tab Menu** button, provides additional options, such as duplicating a particular page, assigning a specific master page, or adding/deleting multiple pages.

To rearrange pages:

- On the **Pages** tab, in the lower **Pages** panel, drag a page thumbnail to a new location in the page sequence.

To add a single page:

1. On the **Pages** tab, click once to select a page in the **Pages** panel.

 The thumbnail that's shown as "selected" is independent of the page you're currently working on. To work on a particular page, double-click its thumbnail.

2. To add a page (or master page) *before* the one selected in the panel, click the ✦ **Add** button.
    OR
    To add a new page *at the end* of the publication, deselect all pages by clicking in the neutral grey region of the lower panel, then click the **Add** button.

If you're using a Serif-supplied Photo Album design template, a dialog lets you base your new page on one of the template's pages or just a blank page. Click on a page and select **OK**.

The page is added to the **Pages** panel. The templates also have alternative single-page layouts that can be adopted.

To add master pages:

For **master pages**, the above procedure applies but within the Master Pages panel. The only exception is that you cannot create a new master page based on a design template's pages (no dialog opens).

For more page/master page insertion options, see "Adding, removing, and rearranging pages" in online Help.

To delete a single page/master page:

1. On the **Pages** tab, select the page (or master page) to delete on the appropriate panel by clicking its thumbnail.

2. Click the ▬ **Delete Page** button.

Setting guides for page margins, rows, columns, and bleeds

Layout guides are visual guide lines that help you position layout elements. They can include **page margins**, **row and column guides**, **bleed area guides**, and **ruler guides**.

Page margin settings are fundamental to your layout, and usually are among the first choices you'll make after starting a publication from scratch. The page margins are shown as a blue box which is actually four guide lines—for top, bottom, left, and right—indicating the underlying page margin settings. If you like, you can set the margins to match your current printer settings.

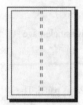

You also have the option of setting up **row** and **column guides** as an underlying layout aid. PagePlus represents rows and columns on the page area with dashed blue guide lines. Unlike the dashed grey **frame margins and columns**, row and column guides don't control where frame text flows. Rather, they serve as visual aids that help you match the frame layout to the desired column layout.

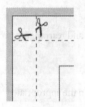

Bleed area guides assist you in positioning "bleed" elements that you want to run to the edge of a trimmed page. To allow for inaccuracies in the trimming process in professional printing, it's a good idea to extend these elements beyond the "trim edge"— the dimensions defined by your Page Setup. With bleed guides switched on, the page border expands by a distance you specify, and the trim edge is shown with dashed lines and little "scissors" symbols. Note that these guide lines are just a visual aid; only the Bleed limit setting in the Print dialog extends the actual output page size.

You can also define free-floating red **ruler guides** on a page by clicking and dragging from the PagePlus rulers. See **Creating ruler guides** on p. 39.

Defining layout guides

To define layout guides:

- Click 🖽 Layout Guides on the Page context toolbar. Then in the **Layout Guides** dialog, use the **Margins** tab as described below.

The **Margins** tab lets you set guide lines for page margins, rows and columns, and bleed areas.

In the **Margin Guides** section, you can set the left, right, top, and bottom margins individually, or click the **From Printer** button to derive the page margin settings from the current printer settings. The dialog also provides options for **balanced margins** (left matching right, top matching bottom) or for **mirrored margins** on facing pages where the "left" margin setting becomes the "inside," and the "right" margin becomes the "outside."

- Use the **Row and Column Guides** section to define guides for rows and columns. If you want rows or columns of uneven width, first place them at fixed intervals, then drag to reposition them as required.

- Use the **Bleed Area Guides** section to specify the extra margin you want to allow around the original Page Setup dimensions or "trim area." Note that if the setting is zero or you have **View>Bleed Area Guides** unchecked, you won't see the bleed area displayed.

To show or hide layout guides:

- On the View menu, check or uncheck **Guide Lines**.

This setting also affects any ruler guides you've placed on the page area. It doesn't affect display of bleed area guides (see below).

To show or hide bleed area guides:

- On the View menu, check or uncheck **Bleed Area Guides**.

Using the rulers and dot grid

The PagePlus **rulers** mimic the paste-up artist's T-square, and serve several purposes:

- To act as a measuring tool

- To create ruler guides for aligning and snapping

- To set and display tab stops (see p. 78)

- To set and display paragraph indents (see p. 77)

Ruler units

To select the basic measurement unit used by the rulers:

- Choose **Options...** from the Tools menu and select the **Rulers** page.

In Paper Publishing mode, the default unit is inches or centimetres; in Web Publishing mode, the default is pixels.

Adjusting rulers

By default, the horizontal ruler lies along the top of the PagePlus window and the vertical ruler along the left edge. The default **ruler intersection** is the top-left corner of the pasteboard area. The default **zero point** (marked as 0 on each ruler) is the top-left corner of the page area. (Even if you have set up **bleed area guides** and the screen shows an oversize page, the zero point stays in the same place, i.e. the top left corner of the trimmed page.)

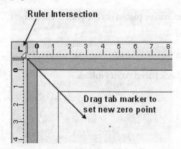

To define a new zero point:

- Drag the tab marker on the ruler intersection to a new zero point on the page or pasteboard. (Be sure to click only the triangular marker!)

To move the rulers:

- With the **Shift** key down, drag the arrow on the ruler intersection. The zero point remains unchanged.

- Double-click on the ruler intersection to make the rulers and zero point jump to the top left-hand corner of the currently selected object. This comes in handy for measuring page objects.

To restore the original ruler position and zero point:

- Double-click the arrow on the ruler intersection.

To lock the rulers and prevent them from being moved:

- Choose **Tools>Options...** and select the **Rulers** page, then check **Lock Rulers**.

Rulers as a measuring tool

The most obvious role for rulers is as a measuring tool. As you move the mouse pointer, small lines along each ruler display the current horizontal and vertical cursor position. When you click to select an object, white ruler regions indicate the object's left, right, top, and bottom edges. Each region has a zero point relative to the object's upper left corner, so you can see the object's dimensions at a glance.

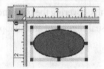

Creating ruler guides

PagePlus lets you to set up horizontal and vertical **ruler guides**—non-printing, red lines you can use to align headlines, pictures, and other layout elements.

Guides are by default "sticky" so that stuck objects can be dragged around the page by their ruler guide—a great way to move previously aligned objects in bulk and simultaneously. You can choose to make objects stick to a guide or unstick them, or even switch sticky guides off completely. (For more details, see **Sticky Guides** on p. 40).

- To create a ruler guide, click on a ruler, hold down your mouse button, then drag onto your page. A red ruler guide line appears parallel to the ruler (**Alt**-click to create the guide at 90 degrees to the ruler).

- To move a guide, drag it.

- To remove a guide, drag and drop it anywhere outside the page area.

- To lock ruler guides, on the **Tools** menu, click **Options...** and select the **Layout** menu option, then check **Lock guide lines**.

- To fine-position ruler guides, choose **Layout Guides...** from the **File** menu (or right-click menu) and select the **Guides** tab. Here, you can create or delete individual guides. To delete all ruler guides at once, click the **Remove All** button.

- To switch off sticky guides, uncheck **Sticky Guides** on the Arrange menu.

- To send guides to the back (for clearer object editing), on the **Tools** menu, click **Options...**, select the **Layout** menu option, then check the **Guide lines to back** option.

Using the dot grid

The **dot grid** is a matrix of dots or lines based on ruler units, covering the page and pasteboard areas. Like ruler guides, it's handy for both visual alignment and snapping.

- To turn the dot grid on or off, click **Dot Grid** on the View menu.
  OR
  Choose **Options...** from the Tools menu and select the **Layout** menu option. Check or uncheck **Dot Grid**.

You can also set the grid spacing, style, colour, and positioning in the dialog (see PagePlus help).

Sticky guides

Guides are normally "sticky" in that objects snapped to them will be moved when the guide is moved across/down the page. Objects stuck to guides can be unstuck individually at any time or the whole feature can be switched off if necessary.

To make individual objects "non-sticky":

1. Select the object.

2. Click one of two small red triangular markers shown at the point where the object is attached to the guide. You'll see a link cursor (⬟) as you hover over the sticky guide marker.

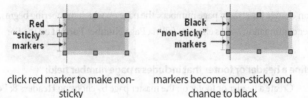

Red → "sticky" markers →

click red marker to make non-sticky

Black → "non-sticky" markers →

markers become non-sticky and change to black

3. If you then drag the red guide away the object will not follow.

You can make the object stick to a guide again by offering it up to the guide line.

To turn sticky guides on and off:

● Check/uncheck **Sticky Guides** from the Arrange menu (or the equivalent from **Tools>Options>Layout**).

Previously stuck objects will remain sticky even after sticky guides are switched off—you'll have to make them non-sticky manually.

Using headers and footers

Headers and footers are layout elements that are positioned at the top and bottom of your master page(s), and are repeated on every page of your publication. The Headers and Footers Wizard lets you create these elements easily.

To create headers and/or footers:

● On the Insert menu, choose **Headers & Footers...** and follow the Wizard instructions. The header and/or footer is automatically applied to the master page (and not the current page).

To edit existing headers and footers:

● Choose **Headers & Footers...** from the Insert menu again, and select "Edit header", "Leave header as it is", or "Delete Header" then complete the wizard. Carry out the equivalent operation for your footer if needed.

Using page numbering

Page number fields automatically display the current page number. Typically, these fields are added automatically to the **master page** (so they appear on every page) with the Header and Footers Wizard, but you can insert a page number field anywhere in your text.

You can change the style of page numbers, the page on which numbering begins, and number continuation across chapters (all via **Page Number Format** on the Format menu).

To define a header or footer that includes a page number field:

1. Create a header or footer on the master page by choosing **Headers & Footers...** from the Insert menu.

2. In the wizard, press the **Page Number** button to insert a page number field (as a prefix or suffix) along with any optional header/footer text, then complete the wizard.

To insert a page number field:

1. In Paper Publishing mode, switch to the master page layer (if desired) by clicking the Current Page box on the HintLine toolbar.

2. Create a new text object. Inside the text object, click for an insertion point to place the page number.

3. On the Insert menu, choose **Page Number**.

Working with Objects

Selecting an object

Before you can change any object, you need to select it using one of these tools from the Tools toolbar:

Pointer Tool

Click to use the **Pointer Tool** to select, move, copy, and resize objects.

Rotate Tool

Click to use the **Rotate Tool** to rotate an object around its centre. Select the object, then drag one of its handles. You can also use the Rotate Tool to move and copy objects. See **Rotating an object**.

To select an object:

- Click on the object using one of the tools shown above. A grey bounding box appears, with small "handles" defining the object's corners and edges.

- If objects overlap, **Alt**-click until the desired object is selected.

When selecting a text object with the Pointer Tool:

- Clicking on a text object with the Pointer tool selects the object and also positions the blinking text selection cursor within the object's text. In this mode, you can edit the text.

- Double-click to select a word, and triple-click to select a paragraph.

- Press the **Delete** key to delete characters after the cursor. To delete the frame itself, choose **Delete Object** from the Edit menu.

To select only the frame (for example, to adjust its margin and column guides), click the frame's bounding box.

Simply clicking on any member of a **group** selects the group object. In general, any operation you carry out on a selected group affects each member of the group. However, you can also select and edit an individual object within a group.

To select an individual object within a group:

- **Ctrl**-click the object.

Selecting multiple objects

Selecting more than one object at a time (creating a **multiple selection**) lets you:

- Position or resize all the objects at the same time.

- Create a **group object** from the multiple selection, which can then be treated as a single object, with the option of restoring the individual objects later. See **Creating Groups** on p. 48.

To create a multiple selection:

- Click in a blank area of the page and drag a "marquee" box around the objects you want to select. Repeated **Shift**-drags add to the selection region.
  OR
  Hold down the **Shift** key and click each object in turn.

To add or remove an object from a multiple selection:

- Hold down the **Shift** key and click the object to be added or removed.

To deselect all objects in a multiple selection:

- Click in a blank area of the page.

To select all objects on the page (or master page):

- Choose **Select All** from the Edit menu (or press **Ctrl+A**).

To select all objects of one type on the page (or master page):

- Hold down the **Ctrl** key and double-click one object of that type.
  OR

- Select one object then choose **Select>Select Similar** on the Edit menu.

To select all objects on a layer:

- Display the Layers tab, choose the layer and right-click to **Select All Objects**.

Snapping

The **snapping** feature simplifies placement and alignment by "magnetizing" grid dots and guide lines. When snapping is on, the edges and centres of objects you create, move, or resize will jump to align with the nearest visible **grid dot** or **guides**. Objects normally snap to the page edge, too.

Guide lines include ruler guides as well as layout guide lines based on page margins, rows, columns, and bleeds (see **Setting guides for page margins, rows, columns, and bleeds** on p. 36).

You may notice that with snapping enabled, when you move a guide, any "snapped to" objects will move with the guide. This object "stickiness" is enabled by default (with the Sticky Guides feature) but can be disabled permanently or temporarily as necessary. It is especially useful for selectively repositioning objects in bulk by guide movement, without any unnecessary grouping operations.

To turn snapping on and off:

- Click the **Snapping** button on the HintLine toolbar. When the button is down, snapping is on.

> Use **Alt**-drag to override snapping temporarily.

Selective snapping

You control which points and lines are snapped to by showing or hiding the individual guide elements (i.e., Rulers, Guide Lines, Frames, Dot Grid, etc.), and by changing options settings for those visible elements.

To show or hide guide elements:

- Check (or uncheck) the element's name on the View menu.
  OR
  Check (or uncheck) the element's name from **Tools>Options>Layout**.
  OR
  Right-click on the page or pasteboard and choose **View**, then select the element's name.

To set which visible elements are snapped to:

1. Choose **Options...** from the Tools menu.

2. Under "Snap to:" on the Layout option, uncheck any elements you don't want to snap to. The choices include **Grid dots**, **Page/Bleed edge**, **Page margins**, **Ruler guides**, **Row/column guides**, **Nearest Pixel**, and **Ruler Marks**.

Creating groups

You can easily turn a **multiple selection** into a group object. When objects are grouped, you can position, resize, or rotate the objects all at the same time.

To create a group from a multiple selection:

- Click the 🔳 **Group** button below the selection.

To ungroup:

- Click the 🔳 **Ungroup** button below the selection to turn back to a multiple selection.

Simply clicking on any member of a group selects the group object. In general, any operation you carry out on a selected group affects each member of the group. However, the objects that comprise a group are intact, and you can also select and edit an individual object within a group.

To select an individual object within a group:

- **Ctrl**-click the object.

Copying, pasting, and duplicating objects

Besides using the Windows Clipboard to copy and paste objects, you can duplicate objects easily using drag-and-drop, and **replicate** multiple copies of any object in precise formations. You can also **transfer the formatting** of one object to another, with the option of selecting specific attributes to be included when formatting is pasted.

To copy an object (or multiple selection) to the Windows Clipboard:

- Click the 📋 **Copy** button on the Standard toolbar.

If you're using another Windows application, you can usually copy and paste objects via the Clipboard.

To paste an object from the Clipboard:

- Click the 📋 **Paste** button on the Standard toolbar.

The standard Paste command inserts the object at the insertion point or (for a separate object) at the centre of the page. To insert a separate object at the same page location as the copied item, use the **Paste in Place** command (**Ctrl+Alt+V**).

To choose between alternative Clipboard formats:

- Choose **Paste Special...** from the Edit menu.

(For details on resizing standard-format pictures, see "Defining the size of pasted pictures" below.)

To duplicate an object:

1. Select the object, then press the **Ctrl** key.

2. Drag the outline to a new location on the page. You can release the **Ctrl** key once you've started the drag.

3. To constrain the position of the copy (to same horizontal or vertical), press and hold down the **Shift** key while dragging. A duplicate of the object appears at the new location.

Replicating objects

Duplicating an object means making just one copy at a time. The **Replicate** command lets you create multiple copies in a single step, with precise control over how the copies are arranged, either as a linear series or a grid. You can include one or more transformations to produce an interesting array of rotated and/or resized objects. It's great for repeating backgrounds, or for perfectly-aligned montages of an image or object.

To replicate an object:

1. Select the object to be replicated and choose **Replicate...** from the Edit menu. The Replicate dialog appears, with a preview region at the right.

2. To arrange copies in a straight line, select **Create line**. For an X-by-Y grid arrangement, select **Create grid**.

3. Specify **Line length** (the number of objects including the original) in the arrangement, or the Grid size. Note that you can use the Line length setting to include an odd number of objects in a grid.

4. Set spacing between the objects as either an **Offset** (measured between the top left corners of successive objects) or a **Gap** (between the bottom right and top left corners). You can specify **Horizontal** and/or **Vertical** spacing, and/or an angular **Rotation**. To set a specific horizontal or vertical interval, check **Absolute**; uncheck the box to specify the interval as a percentage of the original object's dimensions.

5. Click **OK**.

The result is a multiple selection. Click its 🔲 **Group** button if you want to keep the separate objects linked for additional manipulations.

Pasting an object's formatting

Once you have copied an object to the Clipboard, you can use the **Paste Format** to apply its formatting attributes to another object. **Paste Format Plus** displays a "master control" dialog that lets you select or deselect specific attributes to be included when formatting is pasted. See the PagePlus Help for more information on the Paste Format Plus feature.

To paste one object's formatting to another:

1. Copy the source object.

2. Select the target object and choose **Paste Format** from the Edit menu (or press **Ctrl+Shift+V**).

The target object takes on any formatting attributes and settings of the source object that are currently defined in Paste Format Plus.

Moving objects

To move an object (including a multiple selection):

- Click within the object (not on a handle) and drag it to the new location while holding down the left mouse button.
  OR
  Drag the object's grey bounding box.

The view automatically re-centres itself as you drag objects to the edge of the screen.

In Multipage view, you can drag and drop objects between pages. Use the
Multipage button on the View toolbar to set up a convenient viewing mode.

To constrain the movement of an object to horizontal or vertical:

- Select the object and use the keyboard arrows (up, down, left, right).
  OR
  Press and hold down the **Shift** key after you begin dragging the object.

  Release the **Shift** key after you release the left mouse button.

  If you're looking for absolute positioning, you can move objects precisely with the
  Transform tab (See PagePlus Help).

Resizing objects

PagePlus provides several methods of resizing objects. Click-and-drag is the simplest—
watch the HintLine for context-sensitive tips and shortcuts! For extremely precise
resizing, use the Transform tab.

 To set two or more objects to the same horizontal or vertical size as the last
selected object, you can use **Arrange>Size Objects...**.

To resize an object (in general):

1. Select the object.

2. Click one of the selection handles and drag it to a new position while holding
   down the left mouse button.

Dragging from an edge handle resizes in one dimension, by moving that edge. Dragging
from a corner handle resizes in two dimensions, by moving two edges, while
maintaining the selection's aspect ratio (if needed).

 Text in frames and tables doesn't change size when the container object is
resized.

To resize freely:

- Drag from a corner (or line end) handle.

To constrain a shape, frame object, or table object when resizing:

- Hold the **Shift** key down and drag from a corner (or line end) handle.

Resizing groups

You can resize a group object. The size of images, graphic objects, and text objects in the group will change. The size of text inside frames or tables won't change, only the size of the text container.

> You can move, but cannot resize, a multiple selection. Turn the multiple selection into a group first, by clicking the **Group** button below the selection.

If you're looking for absolute control, you can resize objects precisely with the Transform tab (See PagePlus Help).

Locking an object's size or position

To prevent accidentally moving, resizing, flipping, or rotating an object, you can lock it in position.

To lock an object:

- Right-click on the object and choose **Arrange>Lock Objects**, or select the command from the Arrange menu.

To unlock an object:

- Right-click on it and choose **Arrange>Unlock Objects**, or choose the command from the Arrange menu.

Ordering objects

Each new page or master page consists of a single layer. One layer may be enough to accommodate the elements of a particular layout, but you can create additional layers as needed. On each layer, objects such as text frames and pictures are **stacked** in the order you create them, from back to front, with each new object in front of the others. You can change the stacking order, which affects how objects appear on the page.

To change the object's position in the stacking order:

- Select the object.

Then:

- To shift the selected object's position to the bottom of the stack, use the ⬚ **Send to Back** button on the Arrange toolbar.

- To shift the selected object's position to the top of the stack, use the ⬛ **Bring to Front** button on the Arrange toolbar.

- To shift the object's position one step toward the front, right-click on the object and choose **Arrange>Forward One**.

- To shift the object's position one step toward the back, right-click on the object and choose **Arrange>Back One**.

Aligning and distributing objects

Precise **alignment** is one key to a professional layout. You can align the edges of any two or more objects with one another, space them out at certain intervals, or align objects with a page margin. In addition, layout tools such as **rulers** and the **dot grid** provide guides to assist you in placing objects on the page. **Snapping** lets you align objects against sticky or non-sticky guides.

To align the edges of two or more objects:

1. Using the Pointer Tool, **Shift**-click on all the objects you want to align, or draw a marquee box around them, to create a multiple selection.

2. Select the Align tab.
   OR
   Click the ⬛ **Align Objects** button on the Arrange toolbar (or choose **Align Objects...** from the Arrange menu or right-click submenu).

3. In the Align tab or dialog, select an option for vertical and/or horizontal alignment. Choose **Top**, **Bottom**, **Left**, **Right**, **Centre Vertically** or **Centre Horizontally**.

4. Alternatively, to distribute the objects, you can choose **Space Evenly Down** or **Space Evenly Across** to spread selected objects uniformly down or across the either the whole page or by a set measurement (check **Spaced** and set a value in any measurement unit).

To align one or more objects with the page margins:

- Follow the steps above, but check **Include margins**. (If only one object is selected, the option is checked by default.)

Rotating an object

You can rotate objects, including pictures, text objects and groups. (You cannot rotate a multiple selection.)

To rotate an object:

1. Select the **Rotate Tool** on the Tools toolbar.

2. Click to select the object, hover over one of its handles until you see the rotate pointer (below). The object rotates about its centre.

3. Hold the mouse button down and drag the pointer in the direction in which you want to rotate the object, then release (use the **Shift** key for 15° rotation intervals).

To undo rotation (restore the original orientation):

- Double-click the object.

- To restore the rotated position, double-click again.

To rotate an object 90 degrees left or right:

- Select the object and click the ![icon] **Rotate Left** or ![icon] **Rotate Right** button on the Standard toolbar.

To fine-tune rotation:

1. Display the Transform tab and set an Anchor point on the object to be rotated by dragging the blue **Anchor Centre** within the anchor frame or clicking a grey square; the object's rotation will be carried out from that point on the object. For example, an object can be rotated from its bottom-left corner, with the anchor point set accordingly:

2. Using the ⟳ **Rotation Angle** control, rotate the object by a specified amount (in degrees) according to the previously set anchor point position.

Flipping an object

You can flip objects horizontally (left to right; top and bottom stay the same) or
vertically (top to bottom; left and right stay the same).

To flip an object horizontally/vertically:

- Select the object and choose **Flip Horizontal** or **Flip Vertical** from the Arrange
  menu.

To prevent an object from accidentally being flipped:

- Right-click on the object and check **Arrange>Lock Objects**.

Cropping and combining objects

Cropping means masking (hiding) parts of an object or group, for example to improve
composition or create a special effect. The underlying object remains intact.

Several cropping techniques are available to the user:

- You can use either the **Square** or **Irregular Crop Tool** to adjust the object's crop
  outline.

- Use the **Crop to Shape** command, which lets you crop one object to the outline of
  another.

- Objects other than inline pictures have a **wrap outline** which determines how text
  flows around the object. You can adjust this independently of the crop outline.

- The **Combine Curves** command, like Crop to Shape, starts with more than one
  object, but creates a special composite object with one or more "holes" on the inside
  where the component objects' fills overlapped one another—useful for creating
  mask or stencil effects.

- You can **rotate** a cropped object.

To crop using the object's original outline:

1. Select the object, then select the ⊡ **Square Crop Tool** on the Attributes
   toolbar's Crop flyout.

2. Drag one of the object's edge or corner handles inward.

To crop by modifying the object's outline:

- Select the object and select the ⬚ **Irregular Crop Tool** on the Attributes toolbar's Crop flyout. The Curve context toolbar appears, and you'll see the nodes and connecting segments that define the object's crop outline.

- To move a node (control point) where you see the ⊹ cursor, drag the node.

- To move a line segment (between two nodes) where you see the ➤∿ cursor, drag the segment.

- To convert an outline from straight lines to curves, click the ◎ **Fit Curves** button on the Curve context toolbar.

- To adjust the curvature of a segment, drag the control handle(s) of the adjacent nodes.

- ⬚ ⬚ To add or delete nodes for more or less complex outlines, select a node and click the **Add Node** or **Delete Node** button on the Curve context toolbar.

To scroll the visible portion of a cropped object within the crop outline:

- Select the object and drag its centre.

To resize objects within the crop outline:

- Select the object and with the Square Crop Tool enabled, **Ctrl**-drag either upwards or downwards to increase or decrease object size, respectively.

To uncrop (restore full visibility):

- Click the ⬚ **Remove Crop** button on the Attributes toolbar's Crop flyout.

Cropping one shape to another

The **Crop to Shape** command works with exactly two objects selected. Either or both of these may be a group object. The lower object (the one behind the other) gets clipped to the outline of the upper object, leaving a shape equivalent to the overlapping region. Note that you can't crop a **mesh-warped object**, but can use one to crop another object. Use **Combine Curves** to use one shape to punch a "hole" in another.

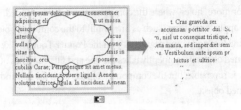

To crop one shape to another:

1. Place the "clipping" object in front of the object to be cropped, using the Arrange menu and/or Arrange toolbar as needed. In the illustration above, a QuickShape is in front of a text frame.

2. Choose **Crop to Shape** from the Tools menu to cut out the obscured underlying text.

You can restore an object cropped in this way to its original shape, but the upper "cropping" object is permanently deleted (use **Undo** to recover it if necessary).

To restore the cropped object to its original shape:

- Click the Remove Crop button on the Attributes toolbar's Crop flyout.

Cropping to the wrap outline

Objects other than inline pictures have a **wrap outline** which determines how text flow changes if the object overlaps a text frame. Initially the wrap outline is set to match the crop outline, but for adjustment purposes the two are independent unless you specify that the crop outline should match the wrap outline. If you're planning to wrap text around an object and also need to crop it somewhat, it will save effort to adjust the wrap outline first, then set the crop outline to match.

To crop a selected object to its wrap outline:

1. Click the Wrap Settings... button on the Arrange toolbar.

2. Check the **Crop object to wrap outline** box.

For details, see **Wrapping text to an object** on p . 97.

Combining lines and shapes

Combining curves is a way of creating a composite object from two or more lines or drawn shapes. As with cropping to a shape, the object in front clips the object(s) behind, in this case leaving one or more "holes" where the component objects overlapped. As with **grouping**, you can apply formatting (such as line or fill) to the combined object and continue to edit individual nodes and segments with the Pointer Tool. Unlike those other methods, a combined object permanently takes the line and fill properties of the front object. Combining is reversible, but the component objects keep the line and fill properties of the combined object.

Combining is a quick way to create a mask or stencil cut-out:

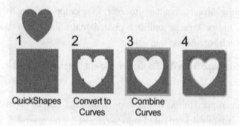

QuickShapes   Convert to   Combine
               Curves   Curves

To combine two or more selected lines or drawn shapes:

1. Draw your two lines or QuickShapes.

2. Place the "clipping" object in front of the object to be cut out, using the Arrange menu and/or Arrange toolbar as needed.

3. Select each object and choose **Tools>Convert to Curves** for both.

4. Select both objects.

5. Choose **Combine Curves** from the Arrange menu.

To restore the original shapes from a combined object:

• Select it and choose **Split Curves** from the Arrange menu.

Applying a mesh warp envelope

Mesh warping lets you define a flexible grid of points and lines that you can drag to deform or distort an object and (optionally) its fill. After applying a basic mesh warp envelope from the Attributes toolbar's Mesh Warp flyout, you can use the **Mesh Warp context toolbar** to switch the warp on/off, edit the mesh by varying its curvature and even custom-design a mesh to match a particular object's geometry—for example, curves that follow the facial contours in a bitmap image—for more precise control of the warp effect. The effect is removable and doesn't permanently alter the object. Note that you can't crop a mesh-warped object, but can use one to crop another object (see **Cropping and combining objects** on p. 55).

The process of editing mesh warps and their envelopes is described in greater detail in the PagePlus Help.

Adding borders

A **border** is a repeating, decorative element that can be set to enclose an object. Borders work especially well with imported pictures.

 TIP: You can adopt ready-made bordered picture frames by using Gallery tab presets.

To add a border to an object:

1. Click the ⬛ **Line/Border** button on the Tools toolbar's Fill flyout.

2. To apply the border to specific edges of the object, use the **Border Edges** tab.

   - To select all edges or no edges, click the corresponding icon in the top row.

   - To toggle a single edge, click the corresponding icon in the bottom row.

   The preview at the left indicates with bolding which edges of the selected object will be updated with the current **Border** tab settings when you click **OK**.

3. To define the border, select the **Border** tab. In the **Side** list, select a border preset. You can preview each border in the window at the right. To remove a border, select **None**.

4. To match the corner pattern to the sides, leave **Keep side and corners the same** checked. To mix and match, uncheck the box and select a preset from the **Corner** list.

5. Choose an **Alignment** setting to fit the border to the **Outside**, **Inside**, or **Middle** of the object's bounding box.

6. Set other properties as needed:

   - To vary the border width, select or type a value in the **Weight** list.

   - If **Behind contents** is checked, the inner half of the border extends behind the object. If unchecked, the whole border appears in front (the wider the border, the more it encroaches on the filled region).

   - If **Scale with object** is checked, both border and object change together when you resize the object. If unchecked, the border weight remains constant during resizing.

7. Click **OK** when you're done.

Working with Text

5

Importing text from a file

Importing text from a word-processor file is the traditional way to create text content for Desktop Publishing layouts (but you can also create a story using WritePlus). If you use your current word processor (such as Microsoft Word) to create the text file for your publication, you can import any number of files into one publication. Each file becomes a **story** consisting of a self-contained section of text like a single article in a newspaper, which resides in one or more linked **text frames**.

 PagePlus will preserve the formatting of imported word-processor text. However, if you're using your word processor to create text specifically for PagePlus, you'll save time by typing as text only, and applying formatting later in PagePlus.

Other methods exist to import textual content—**insert text from a PDF file** using **PDF File...** from the Insert menu (see p. 23). Alternatively, insert a PagePlus file using **PagePlus File...** again from the Insert menu (see p. 22). For now, we'll concentrate on importing text from a text file (typically from a word processor).

To import text from a file:

1. Choose **Text File...** from the Insert menu, or right-click an existing frame and choose **Text File....** The **Open** dialog appears.

2. Select the format of the source file to be imported and locate the file itself. (See below for details on setting the preferred text import format.)

3. Check the "Retain Format" box to retain the source file's formatting styles. Uncheck the box to discard this information. In either case, PagePlus will preserve basic character properties like italic, bold, and underline, and paragraph properties like alignment (left, centre, right).
    For details on how PagePlus handles text styles, see **Using text styles** on p .90.

4. Check the "Ignore Line Wrapping" box to ignore returns in the source text— that is, only if the file has been saved with a carriage return at the end of every line, and you want to strip off these extra returns. Otherwise, leave the box unchecked.

5. Click **OK.**

PagePlus will import the designated text into the pre-selected text object or a new text frame.

Setting the preferred text import format

PagePlus supports direct text import from a number of major word processing applications. Direct import means that in order to import files of a particular format, the word processing application itself must be present on your machine. During installation, PagePlus checks for an installed word processor. You can change the preferred setting to any of the supported applications.

To designate the preferred text import format:

1.   Choose **Options...** from the Tools menu.

2.   On the **General** page, select your preferred word processor in the "Import text using" drop-down list.

If you find that PagePlus does not list your word processor, or if text import from the designated application fails, choose the "Standard Converters" setting, which provides additional formats.

Understanding text frames

Typically, text in PagePlus goes into **text frames**, which work equally well as containers for single words, standalone paragraphs, or multipage articles or chapter text. You can also use **artistic text** (see p. 70) for standalone text with special effects, or **table text** (see Creating text-based tables on p. 109) for row-and-column displays.

What's a text frame?

A text frame is effectively a mini-page, with:

*   Margins and column guides to control text flow

*   Optional preceding and following frames

*   Text and optional **inline images** that flow through the frame (from the previous frame and on to the next).

The text in a frame is called a **story**.

*   When you move a text frame, its story text moves with it.

*   When you resize a text frame, its story text reflows to the new dimensions.

Frames can be linked so that a single story continues from one frame to another. But text frames can just as easily stand alone. Thus in any publication, you can create text in a single frame, spread a story over several frames, and/or include many independent frame sequences. By placing text frames anywhere, in any order, you can build up newspaper or newsletter style publications with many stories flowing from one page to another.

When you select a frame you'll see its bounding box, indicated by a grey border line plus corner and edge handles, and (if you clicked with the Pointer tool) a blinking insertion point in the frame's text. In this mode, you can edit the text with the Pointer tool. As in a word processor, double-clicking selects a word, and triple-clicking selects a paragraph. (For details, see Editing text on the page on p .75)

Text frames behave like other PagePlus objects-you can resize, move, and even crop or rotate them. You can also apply line, fill, and transparency properties to frames. For some operations, it's more convenient if you get rid of the text insertion point and select only the frame.

To select only the frame (no insertion point):

- Click the frame's bounding box.

When only the frame is selected, you can move it more easily. And only in this mode can you directly adjust the frame **margin and column guides** (which constrain the flow of text), as described in **Frame setup and layout** below.

To move a text frame:

- Drag the frame's bounding box.
  OR
  Use the ˣ or ʸ options in the Transform tab.

To resize a text frame:

- In any selection mode, drag a corner or edge handle.
  OR
  Use the ʷ or ᴴ options in the Transform tab.

Creating text frames

You add frames to a page as you would any other object. PagePlus supports a wide variety of frame shapes. You can resize any frame, but cannot alter its basic shape.

To create a frame:

1. Click the 🖳 **Standard Frame Tool** button on the Tools toolbar (for a standard rectangular frame).
    OR
    Click the 🖲 **Shaped Frame Tool** button (its icon displays the most recently selected shape) and select a shape from the flyout submenu.

2. Click on the page or pasteboard to create a new frame at a default size. Drag to adjust the frame's dimensions.

To create a frame (from a shape):

*   You can also draw a shape and select **Convert to Shaped Frame** on the Tools menu (text is not auto-aligned).
    OR

*   Type directly onto any shape to automatically create a shaped frame (text is automatically centred vertically and horizontally). Useful for creating objects for diagrams!

To delete a frame:

*   Select the frame—click its edge until a grey border appears—and then press the **Delete** key. (If there's a selection point in the text, pressing **Delete** will remove characters after the cursor.)

Putting text into a frame

You can put text into a frame using one of the following methods:

1 WritePlus story editor:

*   Right-click on a frame and choose **Edit Story** (**Ctrl+E** with text selected) to start **WritePlus**, PagePlus's integrated story editor.

2 Importing text:

*   Right-click on a frame and choose **Insert Text File...** (**Ctrl+T**) to import text.

3 Typing into the frame:

- Select the **Pointer** tool, then click for an insertion point to type text straight into a frame, or edit existing text. (See **Editing text on the page** on p. 75).

4 Pasting via the Clipboard:

- Select the **Pointer** tool and click for an insertion point in the text, then press **Ctrl+V**.
  Tip: Using the **Edit>Paste Special...** command gives you a choice of formatting options.

5 Drag and drop:

- Select text (e.g. in a word processor file), then drag it onto the PagePlus page.

  If you drop onto a selected frame, the text is pasted inline at the current text insertion point. Otherwise, a new frame is created for the text.

Frame setup and layout

The **frame layout** controls how text will flow in the frame. The frame can contain multiple **columns**. When a frame is selected (and the Frames option is switched on in the View menu), its column margins appear as dashed grey guide lines if set in Frame Setup. Note that unlike the **page margin and row/column guides**, which serve as layout guides for placing page elements, the frame column guides actually determine how text flows within each frame. Text won't flow outside the column margins.

You can drag the column guides or use a dialog to adjust the top and bottom **column blinds** and the left and right **column margins**.

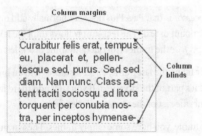

To edit frame properties directly:

- Select the frame object, then drag column guide lines to adjust the boundaries of the column.

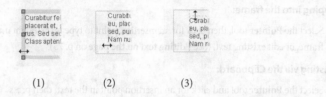

(1)   (2)   (3)

The illustration above shows how the cursor will change when hovering over the bounding box (1), after dragging inwards the column margin can be adjusted (2), and after dragging downwards, the top margin blind can be moved.

To edit frame properties using a dialog:

1. Select the frame and click the ![icon] **Frame Setup** button on the Frame context toolbar.

2. From the dialog, you can change the **Number of columns**, **Gutter** distance between columns, **Left Margin**, **Right Margin**, and enable/disable text wrapping around an object.

3. To change the column widths and blinds (top and bottom frame margins), click a cell in the table and enter a new value.

How a story flows through a sequence of frames

You can have just one frame on its own, or you can have many frames. Frames can be connected in linked **sequences**.

The **story** associated with a given frame sequence flows through the first frame on to the next and keeps flowing into frames in the link sequence.

A key difference from a word processor is that PagePlus does not normally add or remove frames according to the amount of text. The text simply flows until the text runs out (and some frames are left empty), or the frames run out (and some text is left over).

If there is still more text to go after filling the last frame, PagePlus stores it in an invisible **overflow area**, remembering that it's part of the story text. If you later add more frames or reduce the size of text in a frame, the rest of the story text is flowed in.

If the text runs out before the last frame, you have some empty frames. These frames will be filled with text if you add more text to the story, or if you increase the size of the story text.

You can use the **AutoFit** function or the frame's **AutoFlow** button to scale a story's text size so it fits exactly into the available frames. See **Fitting text to frames** on p. 96.

PagePlus keeps track of multiple linked frame sequences, and lets you flow several stories in the same publication. The **Text Manager** (accessed via the Tools menu) provides an overview of all stories and lets you choose which one you want to edit.

Linking text frames

When a text frame is selected, the frame includes a Link button at the bottom right which denotes the state of the frame and its story text, and which allows you to control how the frame's story flows to following frames:

No Overflow

The frame is not linked to a following frame (it's either a standalone frame or the last frame in a sequence) and the end of the story text is visible.

Overflow

The frame is not linked (either standalone or last frame) and there is additional story text in the overflow area. An ⊞ **AutoFlow** button also appears to the left of the Link button.

Continued

The frame is linked to a following frame. The end of the story text may be visible, or it may flow into the following frame.
Note: The button icon will be red if the final frame of the sequence is overflowing, or green if there's no overflow.

There are two basic ways to set up a linked sequence of frames:

- You can link a sequence of empty frames, then import the text.
  OR
  You can import the text into a single frame, then create and link additional frames into which the text automatically flows.

When frames are created by the **AutoFlow** option (for example when importing text), they are automatically linked in sequence.

To create a link or reorder the links between existing frames, you can use the **Link** button or the controls on the Frame context toolbar. Remember to watch the cursor, which changes to indicate these operations...

To link the selected frame to another frame as the next frame:

- Click the frame's ⬚ **Link** button.
  OR
  Select the frame, then click the ⬚ **Link Frame** button on the Frame context toolbar.

- Click with the Textflow cursor on the frame to be linked to. Only empty frames are valid frames to link to.

To unlink the selected frame from the sequence:

- Click the ⬚ **Unlink Frame** button on the Frame toolbar.
  OR
  Click on the frame's **Link** button, then click with the Textflow cursor on the same frame.

Story text remains with the "old" frames. For example, if you detach the second frame of a three-frame sequence, the story text remains in the first and third frames, which are now linked into a two-frame story. The detached frame is always empty.

To navigate from frame to frame:

- Click the ⬚ **Previous Frame** or ⬚ **Next Frame** button on the Frame context toolbar.

Using artistic text

Artistic text is standalone text you type directly onto a page. Especially useful for headlines, pull quotes, and other special-purpose text, it's easily formatted with the standard text tools but has some artistic advantages over frame text. For example, you can initially "draw" artistic text at a desired point size, and drag it to adjust the size later. Unlike the characters in a text frame, an artistic text object can take different line styles, fills (including gradient and Bitmap fills), and transparency for stunning pictorial effects. You can flip artistic text and it will remain editable. And artistic text can even be made to flow along a **curved path** for uniquely creative typographic effects!

To create artistic text:

1. Choose the **Artistic Text Tool** from the Artistic Text flyout on the Tools toolbar.

2. Click on the page for an insertion point using a default point size, or drag to specify a particular size as shown here.

3. Set initial text properties (font, style, etc.) as needed before typing, using the Text context toolbar, Format menu, or right-click (and choose **Text Format**).

4. Type directly on the page to create the artistic text.

Once you've created an artistic text object, you can select, move, resize, delete, and copy it just as you would with a text frame.

To resize or reproportion an artistic text object:

- To resize while maintaining the object's proportions, drag the resize handles.
  OR
  To resize freely, hold down the **Shift** key while dragging.

To edit artistic text:

- Drag to select a range of text; double-click to select a word; or triple-click to select a paragraph.

  Now you can type new text, apply character and paragraph formatting, edit the text in WritePlus, apply proofing options, and so on.

Putting text on a path

"Ordinary" straight-line **artistic text** is far from ordinary—but you can extend its creative possibilities even further by flowing it along a curved path. The resulting object has all the properties of artistic text, plus its path is a Bézier curve that you can edit with the Pointer Tool as easily as any other line! In addition, text on a path is editable in some unique ways, as described below.

PagePlus offers four ways to create text on a path, i.e.

To apply a preset curved path to text:

1. Create an artistic text object.
2. With the text object selected, on the Text context toolbar, click the Path flyout and choose a preset path.

The text now flows along the specified path.

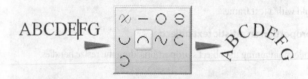

To add artistic text along an existing line or shape:

1. Create a freehand, straight, or curved line (see **Drawing and editing lines** on p. 147) or a shape (see **Drawing and editing shapes** on p. 153).

2. Choose the **A Artistic Text Tool** from the Artistic Text flyout on the Tools toolbar.

3. Bring the cursor very close to the line. When the cursor changes to include a curve, click the mouse where you want the text to begin. The line changes to a dotted line.
   Note: If you don't want to create text on a path, you can override the cursor response by holding down the **Alt** key.

4. Begin typing at the insertion point. Text flows along the line, which has been converted to a path.

To fit existing text to an existing line or shape:

1. Create an artistic text object.

2. Create a freehand, straight, or curved line (see **Drawing and editing lines** on p. 147) or a shape (see **Drawing and editing shapes** on p. 153).

3. Select both objects. On the **Tools** menu, choose **Fit Text to Curve**. The text now flows along the specified path.

To create text and path at the same time:

1. Choose one of the Path Text tools from the Artistic Text flyout:

    The **Freehand Path Text Tool** lets you sketch a curved line in a freeform way

    The **Straight Path Text Tool** is for drawing a straight line

    The **Curved Path Text Tool** lets you join a series of line segments (which may be curved or straight) using "connect the dots" mouse clicks

2. Create a line on the page. Your line appears as a path with an insertion point at its starting end (for a curved path you can either type directly onto any part of the path or press **Esc** or double-click to get the insertion point at the start of the path).

3. Begin typing at the insertion point. Text flows along the path.

Editing text on a path

Artistic text on a path remains editable as text. Likewise, you can continue to edit its path with the Pointer Tool and Curve context toolbar, as described in Drawing and editing lines on p. 147.

When a path text object is selected, you'll notice that text paths have several unique "handles" not found on other objects. You may need to zoom in a bit, but it's easy to select the handles—special cursors let you know when you're directly over them. To see what the handles do, carefully compare these two examples:

- The **Baseline Shift** handle, indicated by a cursor, resembles a QuickShape handle with a tiny slider control. Drag the slider to raise and lower the text with respect to the path. In the right-hand example above, we've lowered the original text.

- The **Start** and **End** handles, indicated by and cursors, look like arrows. Drag them to adjust where the text begins and ends with respect to the path's start and end nodes. In the above example, we've shifted the text to the left by dragging the Start handle.

You can flip text from one side of a path to the other by reversing curves. This switches the start and end nodes of the path, so the text runs in the other direction. It's handy, for example, if you want to move text from the outside to the inside of a circular path, to run counter-clockwise rather than clockwise, or vice versa. Note that the text isn't mirrored—it still reads correctly!

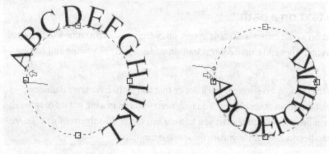

To reverse the text path:

- Select the path text object and click the **Reverse Curves** button on the Curve context toolbar.

Whichever method you used to create a path text object, you can always detach the text as a separate artistic text object by removing its path.

To remove the text path:

1.   Select the path text object.

2.   Click the ⊗ **Path-None** button on the Text context toolbar's Path flyout.

The text remains as a straight-line artistic text object and the path is permanently removed.

Editing text on the page

You can use the Pointer Tool to edit **frame text**, **table text**, or **artistic text** directly. On the page, you can select and enter text, set paragraph indents and tab stops, change text properties, apply text styles, and use **Find and Replace**. For editing longer stories, and for more advanced options, choose WritePlus.

Selecting and entering text

Several methods exist for selection of frame text, artistic text, table text, in fact any type of text you'll encounter in PagePlus. The selection area will be shaded in semi-transparent blue for clear editing.

To select text on the page:

To select...	Action	Example
a single word	double-click	Nulla vestibulum eleifend nulla. Suspendisse potenti. Aliquam turpis nisi, venenatis non, accumsan nec, imperdiet laoreet, lacus.
multiple words	**Ctrl**-click or **Ctrl**-drag	Nulla vestibulum eleifend nulla. Suspendisse potenti. Aliquam turpis nisi, venenatis non, accumsan nec, imperdiet laoreet, lacus.
a paragraph	triple-click	Nulla vestibulum eleifend nulla. Suspendisse potenti. Aliquam turpis nisi, venenatis non, accumsan nec, imperdiet laoreet, lacus.

a portion of text	drag with cursor (use **Ctrl**-drag for multiple portions of text). Use **Shift** key when clicking between two insertion points.	Nulla vestibulum eleifend nulla. Suspendisse potenti. Aliquam turpis nisi, venenatis non, accumsan nec, imperdiet laoreet, lacus.
a box column	**Alt**-drag	Nulla vestibulum eleifend nulla. Suspendisse potenti. Aliquam turpis nisi, venenatis non, accumsan nec, imperdiet laoreet, lacus.

You can multi-select identical words and phrases by using the **Find and Replace's Select All** feature (see p. 81).

To edit text on the page:

*   Select the Pointer Tool, then click (or drag) in the text object. A standard insertion point appears at the click position (see below), or if a single word, paragraph or portion of text is already selected (see above), type to replace the selected text.

    Nulla vestibulum eleifend nulla. Suspendisse potenti. Aliquam turpis nisi, venenatis non, accumsan nec, imperdiet laoreet, lacus.

To start a new paragraph:

*   Press **Enter**.

To start a new line within the same paragraph (using a "line break" or "soft return"):

*   Press **Shift+Enter**.

The following three options apply only to frame text. You can use these shortcuts or choose the items from the **Insert/Break** submenu.

To flow text to the next column (Column Break), frame (Frame Break) or page (Page Break):

*   Press **Ctrl+Enter**, **Alt+Enter** or **Ctrl+Shift+Enter**, respectively.

To switch between insert mode and overwrite mode:

*   Press the **Insert** key.

To repeat a text action:

- Choose **Repeat** from the Edit menu, or press **Ctrl+Y**.

For example, if you've applied new formatting to one paragraph, you can click in another paragraph and use the **Repeat** command to apply the same formatting there.

Copying, pasting and moving text

You can easily copy frame text and paste into the same or a different text frame. Text stored on the clipboard can additionally be pasted into a new frame.

Drag and drop support for frame text allows text to be moved into a different location within the same frame or a different text frame in your publication.

To copy and paste text:

1. Select the text to be copied.

2. Select **Copy** from the Edit menu. This places the text onto the clipboard.

3. Place an insertion point in a different location in your story or artistic text.

4. Select **Paste** from the Edit menu.

If you don't place an insertion point, the text can be pasted into a new text frame directly.

To move text by drag and drop (text frames only):

1. Select the text to be moved.

2. Hover over the selected text and hold your mouse button down. A cursor is shown.

3. Move the cursor to the location (in the same or different frame) you wish to place the text—an insertion point should be displayed.

4. Release the mouse button to place your text.

Setting paragraph indents

When a text object is selected, markers on the horizontal ruler indicate the left indent, first line indent, and right indent of the current paragraph. You can adjust the markers to set paragraph indents, or use a dialog.

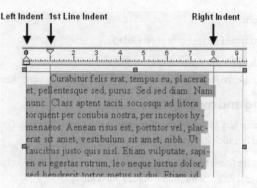

Left Indent 1st Line Indent   Right Indent

- The **Left** indent is set in relation to the object's left margin.

- The **1st line** indent is in relation to the left indent.

- The **Right** indent is in relation to the object's right margin.

For details on setting frame margins, see **Frame setup and layout** (on p. 67).

To set the indents of the current paragraph:

- Drag the appropriate ruler marker(s).
  OR

  For quick left indents, select the 🔲 **Increase Level** or 🔲 **Decrease Level** button to increase or decrease indent, respectively. Indent is by the currently set default tab stop distance.
  OR

  To adjust indent settings numerically, choose **Paragraph...** from the Format menu (or **Text Format>Paragraph...** from the right-click menu). In the Indentation box, you can enter values for Left, Right, 1st Line, or Hanging indents.

Setting tab stops

To set a tab stop:

1. Select the paragraph(s) in which you want to set tab stops.

2. Click the ruler intersection button until it changes to the type of tab you want: (Left, Centre, Right, or Decimal).

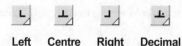

Left   Centre   Right   Decimal

3. Click on the horizontal ruler where you want to set a tab stop.

- To move a tab stop, drag it to a new ruler position.

- To delete a tab stop, drag it off the ruler.

> If you want to set precise measurements for tabs, right-click the frame and choose **Text Format**, then select **Tabs...** from the submenu.

Sorting text

PagePlus lets you sort words, numbers or a combination of both. The sorting mechanism is paragraph based so it's just as easy to sort whole paragraphs as well as single letters if necessary—it's all the same to PagePlus! Sorting can be carried out in ascending (A to Z, or 0 to 9) or descending order (Z to A, or 9 to 0) to a set priority: punctuation marks first, then numbers, letters, and symbols last.

Intelligent sorting takes place when a dealing with lists comprising weekdays and months. Rather than order by first letter, the sort can be carried out by weekday or month order instead.

To sort text:

1. Select the artistic text or text frame containing the text to be sorted. Alternatively, drag across over a portion of text to create a text selection to which sorting is limited to.

2. Select the ⬇️ **Sort** button from the Text context toolbar.

3. From the dialog, choose a **Sort** method. Typically, you would choose Normal but if your list contains weekdays or months, pick a date format from the **Sort** drop-down menu which matches your list's date format. This will then sort on month order rather than alphabetic order.

4. Enable either the **Ascending** or **Descending** button.

5. Check **Case Sensitive** to separate out lower case characters from upper case characters (which list first).

6. To check **Treat numbers as text** to order number lists as 1, 10, 12, 3, 5 instead of 1, 3, 5, 10, 12.

Working with Unicode text

PagePlus fully supports Unicode, making it possible to incorporate foreign characters or special symbols.

- To paste Unicode text from the Clipboard to the page, use **Edit/Paste Special...**.

- Insert Unicode characters directly into your text by typing your Unicode Hex value and pressing Alt-X. The Alt-X keyboard operation toggles between the displayed character (e.g., @) and its Hex value (e.g., U+0040) equivalent. See Inserting Unicode characters.

- To export text in Unicode format, use WritePlus.

Editing story text with WritePlus

WritePlus is the story editor built into PagePlus. For certain tasks, such as viewing and editing the full text of an entire story that may be spread over many frames or pages, it's much more convenient than **Editing text on the page**. And for other tasks, such as exporting story text or **Marking index entries**, it's essential!

> You can also use WritePlus to edit artistic text, but not table text.

To launch WritePlus:

- Right-click on a text frame or artistic text object and choose **Edit Story** (or with text selected, press **Ctrl+E** or choose **Edit Story** from the Edit menu). WritePlus opens with the object's story text.

The WritePlus environment

WritePlus opens in a separate window that shares many of the standard PagePlus menus and toolbars. As you make changes in WritePlus, story text in the main window updates instantly.

The WritePlus workspace can have one or two windows. Initially, you'll see the **Text Entry window**.

To display a **Style Pane** on the left, click the **Style Pane** button, revealing style names such as "Normal" and "Heading 1" (if applied).

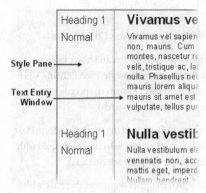

Style Pane →

Text Entry Window →

By default, WritePlus opens in **Layout Mode**, displaying text with formatting applied. You can quickly switch to **Draft Mode**, which doesn't display formatting variations.

To switch between Draft Mode and Layout Mode:

- Click the ◢ **Formatting** button on the Story toolbar.

The Story toolbar, unique to WritePlus, includes other tools to assist you in working with story text. For example, the **Story list** lets you select the story to be edited, or change the name of a story by typing in the list. Click the **Word Count** button to run a wizard that counts total words or characters, toggle any fields, or view the number of occurrences of a specified word.

To close WritePlus and return to PagePlus:

- Click the ✔ **Finish** button or the window's ⊠ Close button.

Using Find and Replace

You can search publication text for an extraordinary variety of items: not just words or parts of words, but a host of character and paragraph attributes such as fonts, styles, alignment, bullets and numbering, missing fonts, drop caps... ... even inline graphics and more! Using the Find and Replace dialog—which remains open without interrupting your work until you click its **Close** button—you can replace globally, or on a case-by-case basis.

To use Find and Replace:

1. Choose **Find & Replace...** from the Edit menu or press **Ctrl+F**.

2. In the dialog, type the text to be found in the **Find** box and its replacement text (if any) in the **Replace** box. Click the down arrows to view recent items. Click either box's button to use flyout menus to select formats or special characters, or define a regular expression (for a wildcard-type search).

3. Select the Range to be searched: **Current Story** (just the currently selected text object or story), or **All Stories** (all text), or **Current Selection** (only used with the Replace All function to operate on the currently selected text).

4. Select **Match whole word only** to match character sequences that have **white space** (space, tab character, page break etc.) or punctuation at each end, or which are at the start/end of a paragraph. Select **Match case** for case-sensitive search. Select **Regular expressions** to treat the contents of the Find box as an expression, rather than as a literal string to be found.

5. Click **Find Next** to locate the first instance of the Find text.
    OR
    Click **Select All** to highlight all instances of matching text in your document simultaneously.

6. Click **Replace** if you want to substitute the replacement text. Alternatively, click **Find Next** again to skip to the next matching text. Continue using the Replace option as required until you reach the end of your document.
    OR
    Click **Replace All** to replace all instances of the Find text with the replacement text at the same time. PagePlus reports when the search is completed.

7. Click **Close** to dismiss the Find and Replace dialog.

The Find and Replace dialog also lets you perform a wildcard-type search by using a **regular expression**—a formula for generating a set of strings—to specify complex search criteria. This is covered in more detail in PagePlus Help.

Inserting footnotes and endnotes

Within **frame text**, it's easy to add **footnotes** (which normally go at the bottom of a column) and/or **endnotes** (normally at the end of a text story). In either case you can customize the consecutive numbering or symbols used by reference marks, the style of both marks and note body text, and the placement and layout of note text, including optional line separators. You can add and view notes either on the page or in WritePlus.

To insert a footnote or endnote:

1.   Click for an insertion point in a text frame. If updating an existing custom mark, select it first. (To view notes in WritePlus, check **Note Pane** on the View menu.)

2.   Choose **Footnote/Endnote...** from the Insert menu.

3.   Select either the **Footnote** or **Endnote** tab.

4.   Set the Number format, Start at, Restart each and Note position fields as appropriate.

PagePlus displays the new footnote/endnote followed by a text edit cursor, so you can immediately enter the text of the note.

Setting text properties

PagePlus gives you a high degree of typographic control over characters and paragraphs, whether you're working with **frame text**, **table text**, or **artistic text**.

To apply basic text formatting:

1.   Select the text.

2.   Use the Text context toolbar to change **font** style, point size, attributes, paragraph alignment and level.
OR

Right-click the text and choose **Text Format**, then select from the submenu: Character... , Paragraph... , Tabs... , Bullets & Numbering... , or Drop Cap... , Kern, or Vertical Alignment. (You can also select these items from the Format menu.)

If a font is unavailable and has been substituted, its font name on the Text context toolbar is prefixed by the "?" character.

Default text properties

Default text properties are the settings used for text you type into any new text object. You can change these settings directly from selected text, or using the **Text Style Palette**. The Palette has the advantage of letting you review all the settings at a glance.

To change default text properties:

1. Create a single sample of text and fine-tune its properties as desired—or use existing text that already has the right properties.

2. Select the text or frame and choose **Update Text Default** from the Format menu.

PagePlus preserves the formatting of imported word-processor text. If you've imported or pasted text and want to apply different formatting, you can first reset the text to use the default text properties.

To clear custom formatting (restore plain/default text properties):

- From the Text Styles tab, select **Clear Formatting** to clear both character and paragraph formatting. Click the drop-down arrow to selectively **Apply to Character** or **Apply to Paragraph**.
  OR
  On the Text context toolbar, click to expand the Text Styles drop-down list and select **Clear Formatting** (to clear both text and paragraph formatting).
  OR
  Select a range of text and then on the Format menu, choose **Clear Text Formatting** (again for both).

The PagePlus Help provides a Text Properties summary for detailed reference.

Using fonts

One of the most dramatic ways to change your document's appearance is to change the fonts used in your artistic or frame text. Applying different fonts to a character or entire paragraph can communicate very different messages to your intended readership.

Lorem Ipsum

LOREM IPSUM

Lorem Ipsum *Lorem Ipsum*

Lorem Ipsum

Font assignment is very simple in PagePlus, and can be done from the **Fonts** tab, Text context toolbar, or in the **Character** dialog (via right-click, or from the Format menu). However, the advantages of using the Fonts tab over the other methods include the ability to:

- hover-over preview of fonts on your document's text.

- assign fonts via single-click.

- search for installed fonts.

- access FontManager (if purchased).

The **Fonts** tab is automatically hidden by default, but can be viewed by clicking the arrow button at the left of your workspace. You may also need to click the **Fonts** label to display the **Fonts** tab.

Assigning and previewing fonts

The fonts shown in the **Fonts** tab represent the currently installed fonts on your computer. This means that these fonts are available to format any selected character or paragraph. you can even associate the font with a **text style**.

> To install/uninstall fonts, and generally manage your fonts, you can use Serif FontManager.

To assign a font:

● Select some text, then click on the font name in the Fonts tab to assign the font to the text.

To recall previously assigned fonts quickly, the last six assigned fonts are displayed in a **Recently used fonts** sub-window at the top of the tab.

You can preview how fonts will appear on your selected text by enabling PagePlus's font preview feature.

To preview fonts:

1. From the tab's ▣ **Tab Menu** button (top-right of tab), check the **Preview Font** option.

2. Select a section of text (a letter, word, or paragraph) in your document.

3. On the **Fonts** tab, hover over any font in the list. The selected text will update to show how the font will appear in situ.

Searching for fonts

While it's handy to see your recently used fonts separate from the other fonts, the **Fonts tab** also hosts an extremely useful search feature which filters your installed fonts in several ways. You can search for an individual font name (in full or part of), or other attributes, as well as multiple fonts simultaneously.

To search for fonts (by name):

1. At the bottom of the **Fonts** tab, click in the **Type to search** window.

2. You can type the full font name or a portion of the font name.

This immediately produces a filtered subset of fonts in the same font list (replacing the fonts previously listed).

Several methods can be used to search for multiple font names. You can use "space" or "comma, followed by space" to perform "AND" or "OR" operations, respectively.

To search for fonts (by attribute):

1. At the bottom of the **Fonts** tab, click the ⌄ Attributes button.

2. In the pop-up list, select an attribute to filter on.

Combined searches

Any combination of strings, made up of text and attributes, can be assembled to filter your fonts. By using the "AND " and "OR" approach, you can create very powerful search criteria. However, a balance must be struck between the complexity of your search and the number of fonts installed. Why create a complex search just to navigate a small number of installed fonts?

Changing common fonts

Changing one font for another is very simple for a single portion of text, but the **Fonts** tab can take things a step further by allowing a font to be located throughout the entire document, and if necessary, swapped for another font. By using the auto-preview feature, it's simple to re-assign a different font to any text the original font was applied to.

To select (and change) a font throughout your document:

1. Right-click a font displayed in the **Fonts** tab.

   If the font is used in your document, you'll see a "*Select All n instance(s)*" message (*n* is the number of times the font is used). If there are no occurrences, you'll get a "*Not currently used*" message.

2. Click the message label—text formatted with the chosen font is selected.

3. Hover over font names in your font list. Click on a chosen font to apply it to the selected text.

Substituting fonts

Font substitution issues may arise when opening PagePlus Publications (*.PPP) and importing PDF files that have no embedded fonts. This is because the fonts used in the original document may not be present on the target PC. If this occurs, font substitution of that unavailable font will be indicated to the user via a dialog as the .PPP or .PDF file is opened—the font status will be "Not Available".

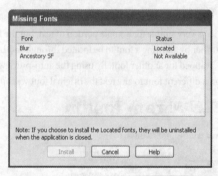

If Serif FontManager is installed, the dialog also lets you manually install fonts which are present on your computer but are currently unavailable because they are uninstalled. This dynamic installation of fonts is only temporary as the font is uninstalled again when PagePlus closes.

Status	Description
Searching	This status may be displayed temporarily as PagePlus locates fonts and their current status.
Located	The fonts associated with your document's text (e.g., Blur) are not installed but they have been located, and are available to be dynamically installed from the dialog (only shown with FontManager installed).
Not Available	The fonts associated with your document's text (e.g., Ancestry SF) are not present on your computer—font substitution will take place automatically after closing the dialog.

Any font that is in your document and already installed on your computer will never be shown in the dialog.

To install fonts dynamically with FontManager installed:

1. Launch Serif PagePlus and open a PagePlus publication (*.PPP). The above dialog will display if font substitution and/or dynamic font installation can occur.

2. Click the **Install** button to dynamically install all fonts with status **Located** (they will uninstall when closing PagePlus). Using the example above, the "Blur" font would be dynamically installed to the Windows Fonts folder (a link is made to the located font's original folder).

When the current session is closed, the dynamically installed fonts will uninstall automatically. The closing of a document will not uninstall its dynamically installed fonts.

Substitution in detail

PagePlus's font substitution mechanism makes use of the PANOSE Font Matching System which intelligently (and automatically) finds the best font substitution match between a missing and a locally available font.

PagePlus will use any embedded TrueType (TTF) fonts and OpenType fonts with TTF or Type 1 outlines in imported PDF to honour the intended appearance of imported text that uses those fonts.

If a font is unavailable and has been substituted, its font name on the context toolbar is prefixed by the "?" character.

After this point, three options are open to you:

●   continue with the fonts already substituted on import.

●   install the original fonts that have been substituted (font substitution will no longer occur).

●   swap the fonts substituted on import with fonts of your choosing.

The last option is carried out via PagePlus's **Resource Manager**, designed for font management. The Fonts tab is used for font substitution via a **Substitute Missing Fonts** dialog.

The dialog allows missing fonts to be substituted by **Available Fonts** selected from a font list. The available fonts are those currently installed on your PC. It's also possible to add more than one font to act as a replacement, which is particularly useful if you want to provide an alternative to your first choice substituted font, e.g. Tahoma could be a primary font substitute and Arial a secondary one (as it's more widely available).

For each font substitution in the **Substitute Missing Fonts** dialog, the mappings shown in the Substitute with box can be reset to default by clicking the **Default** button. This will replace the fonts listed with a single font, e.g. Arial or Times New Roman, as governed by Windows (this is not configurable).

To substitute a font:

1. Select **Resource Manager** from the Tools menu.

2. Choose the **Fonts** tab, and select the **Substitutions** button.

3. In the dialog, select a missing font from the **Font to substitute** drop-down menu.

4. Choose a replacement font from the Available fonts list box ensuring that the **Bold** and/or **Italic** options are checked if necessary. Some fonts may be a more acceptable substitute with the bold or italic style set.

5. Click **Add**<< to place the font in the **Substitute with** box. This box can contain more than one font—your first choice and a secondary font (e.g. Arial or Times New Roman). You should always place your first choice at the top of the list with the **Move up** or **Move down** buttons.

6. Go back to Step 3 and substitute each missing font in the **Font to substitute** drop-down menu in turn.

 TIP: You can export all your saved font substitution to .SFM files for future use. An import feature also exists.

Using text styles

It's a good idea to establish the main text and graphic formatting to be used in your publication early in the creative process. PagePlus facilitates this by letting you define named text styles, which can be applied to **frame text**, **table text**, or **artistic text**. A text style is a set of character and/or paragraph attributes saved as a group. When you apply a style to text, you apply the whole group of attributes in just one step. For example, you could define named paragraph styles for particular layout elements, such as "Heading," "Sidebar," or "Body Text," and character styles to convey meaning, such as "Emphasis,"

"Price," or "Date Reference." Using styles not only speeds the task of laying out a publication but ensures consistency and ease of updating.

Styles can be applied to characters or paragraphs using either the Text context toolbar or the Text Styles tab. Both paragraph and character styles can be managed from the **Text Style Palette**.

Paragraph and character styles

A **paragraph style** is a complete specification for the appearance of a paragraph, including all font and paragraph format attributes. Every paragraph in PagePlus has a paragraph style associated with it.

- PagePlus includes one built-in paragraph style called **"Normal"** with a specification consisting of generic attributes including left-aligned, 12pt Times New Roman. Initially, the "Normal" style is the default for any new paragraph text you type. You can modify the "Normal" style by redefining any of its attributes, and create any number of new styles having different names and attributes.

- Applying a paragraph style to text updates all the text in the paragraph except sections that have been locally formatted. For example, a single word marked as bold would remain bold when the paragraph style was updated.

A **character style** includes only font attributes (name, point size, bold, italic, etc.), and you apply it at the character level—that is, to a range of selected characters—rather than to the whole paragraph.

- Typically, a character style applies emphasis (such as italics, bolding or colour) to whatever underlying font the text already uses; the assumption is that you want to keep that underlying font the same. The base character style is shown in the Text Style Palette simply as "Default Paragraph Font," which has no specified attributes but basically means "whatever font the paragraph style already uses."

- The Default Paragraph Font appears in the Text Styles tab (or the Text context toolbar's Styles box) as "**Clear Formatting**" because applying it strips any local character or paragraph formatting (or both) you've added and restores original text attributes.

- As with paragraph styles, you can define any number of new character styles using different names and attributes. Custom character styles don't usually include a specific font name or point size, but there's no rule against including them.

Working with named styles

The named style of the currently selected text is displayed in either the Text Styles tab or the drop-down **Styles** box on the Text context toolbar. A character style (if one is applied locally) may be shown; otherwise it indicates the paragraph style. You can use either the tab, the drop-down Styles box, or a dialog to apply a particular style to the existing text. The Text Style Palette (accessible from the Text Styles tab) lets you modify an existing style, or define a new style.

By default, a limited set of styles are shown in the Text Styles tab, although you can display all styles by checking the tab's **Show All** option (or via **Tools>Options**; **UI Settings**). The Default Paragraph Font, some common styles, and your document's currently used styles (plus any associated styles) will always be shown. You can preview any style and then apply it to a word, paragraph, or story.

To preview a style:

1. From the tab's ▶ **Tab Menu** button (top-right of tab), check the **Preview Style** option.

2. Select a section of text (a letter, word, or paragraph) in your document.

3. On the **Text Styles** tab, hover over any style in the list (check the **Show All** option to see all styles). The selected text will update to show how the style will appear in situ.

To apply a named style:

1. Using the **Pointer Tool**, click in a paragraph (if applying a paragraph style) or select a range of text (if applying a character style).

2. Display the Text Styles tab and select a style from the style list.
   OR
   On the Text context toolbar, click the arrow to expand the Styles drop-down list and select a style name.

The applied style appears in the tab's style list.

To update a named style using the properties of existing text:

1. Make your desired formatting changes to any text that uses a named style.

2. On the **Text Styles** tab, right-click the style and choose **Update <style> to Match Selection**.
   OR
   On the Text context toolbar, click the arrow to expand the Styles drop-down list and select the current style name again. Click **OK** to confirm the option to "Update the style to reflect recent changes."

All text using the named style, throughout the publication, takes on the new properties.

To create a new style:

1. On the **Text Styles** tab, select the style on which you want your new style to be based and then:
   Click the 🖳 **Create Style** button.
   OR
   Right-click and choose **Base New Style on** <*selected style name*>.

2. In the **Text Style** dialog, define the style **Name**, the style to be **Based On**, **Style for the following paragraph**, and the style to be changed to if **Increase Level** is applied. From the left-hand tree menu change any character or paragraph attributes, tabs, bullets, and drop caps you want to include in the new style definition. Check **Always list in Studio** to ensure the style will always appear in the Text Styles tab.

3. Click **OK** to create the style, or **Cancel** to abandon changes.

To create a new style using the properties of existing text:

1. Format the text as desired.

2. To define a character style, select a range of reformatted text. To define a paragraph style, deselect text but leave a blinking cursor (insertion point) within the newly formatted section.

Type a new style name into the Text context toolbar's Styles box and press **Enter**.

The new style is defined with the properties of the selected text.

To modify an existing style:

1. On the **Text Styles** tab, right-click on the character or paragraph style you want to modify and then choose **Modify** *<style>*....

2. In the **Text Style** dialog, navigate the attribute tree menu, make your modifications, and then click **OK**.

Removing local formatting

To return characters or paragraphs back to their original formatting (Normal style; default paragraph font), use the **Clear Formatting** option. This is great for reverting some formatting which hasn't quite worked out! You can easily remove local formatting from a single word, selected text area, paragraph, or entire story.

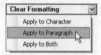

To remove local formatting:

1. Select a locally formatted area of text (double- or triple-click to select a word or paragraph, respectively).

2. On the **Text Styles** tab, click on **Clear Formatting**. This clears both character and paragraph formatting simultaneously (alternatively use **Apply to Both** from the drop-down menu or **Clear Text Formatting** from the Format menu).

   OR

   Select **Apply to Character** to remove all local character formatting (leaving paragraph formatting untouched).

   OR

   Select **Apply to Paragraph** to remove all local paragraph formatting (leaving character formatting untouched).

Like Clear Formatting, you can use **Reapply Styles** on the **Text Styles** tab (or Text context toolbar) to clear all local overrides within a paragraph leaving the default text. However, if text styles are used, the option can be used to maintain the paragraph's original text styles, whilst removing any character or paragraph style overrides, or both. Use **Apply to Character** (retaining paragraph styles overrides), **Apply to Paragraph** (retaining character style overrides) and **Apply to Both** to remove both character or paragraph style overrides simultaneously.

For example, consider a paragraph using the built-in "Body Text" style which has several words within it bolded. Reapplying the "Body" style to the paragraph would not undo the local bold marking. However, selecting the paragraph and applying "Clear Formatting" would set all the text back to regular 10pt Times New Roman. Similarly, paragraph alignment could be set to be right-aligned (overriding the default left alignment), but clear formatting with **Apply to Paragraph** will revert the paragraph style to left alignment again.

Changing common styles

Changing one character or paragraph style for another is very simple for a single portion of text. However, in PagePlus, it's just as easy to swap one style for another by selecting multiple instances of the style and, by using the auto-preview feature, choosing an alternative style. This swaps styles across paragraphs and throughout entire stories all at the same time.

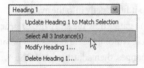

To select (and change) a style throughout your document:

1. Right-click a style displayed on the **Text Styles** tab.

2. If the style is used in your document, you'll see a "*Select All n instance(s)*" message (*n* is the number of times the style is used).

    If there are no occurrences of the style, you'll see a "*Not currently used*" message.

3. Click the message label—text formatted with the chosen style is highlighted.

4. Hover over style names in your styles list. Click on a chosen style to apply the style to the selected text.

Fitting text to frames

Fitting story text precisely into a sequence of frames is part of the art of laying out publications.

If there's too much story text to fit in a frame sequence, PagePlus stores it in an invisible **overflow area** and the Link button on the last frame of the sequence displays ⬚ and an **AutoFlow** appears next to the Link button. You might edit the story down or make more room for it by adding an extra frame or two to the sequence. Clicking the AutoFlow button adds additional frames and pages as needed (see below).

The Frame context toolbar includes several tools that can simplify the task of fitting text to frames:

⊠   **AutoFit**

Click to scale the story's text size so it fits exactly into the available frames. You can use this early on, to gauge how the story fits, or near the end, to apply the finishing touch. AutoFit first applies small point size changes, then small leading changes, then adjustments to the paragraph space below value, until the text fits. Other settings are not affected. (Also see Note below.)

Tip: You can also press **Ctrl+Alt+X** to apply AutoFit.

⊠   **Enlarge Story Text**

Click to increase the story's text size one increment. Click for a bigger increase.

⊠   **Shrink Story Text**

Click to reduce the story's text size one increment. Click for a greater reduction.

AutoFlow

When importing text, it's a good idea to take advantage of the **AutoFlow** feature, which will automatically create text frames and pages until all the text has been imported. This way, enough frames are created to display the whole story. Then you can gauge just how much adjustment will be needed to fit the story to the available "real estate" in your publication.

If you add more text to a story while editing, or have reduced the size of frame, you may find that an overflow condition crops up. In this case (see above) you can decide whether to use AutoFit or click the frame's **AutoFlow** button.

To AutoFlow story text on the page:

- Click the ⬚ **AutoFlow** button just to the left of the frame's ⬚ Link button.

Wrapping text

PagePlus lets you wrap frame text around the contours of a separate object. Usually, this means wrapping text to a picture that overlaps or sits above a text frame. But you can wrap frame text around an artistic text object, a table or another frame, or even flow text inside a graphic (a circle, for example). Wrapping is accomplished by changing the **wrap setting** for the object to which text will wrap.

Wrap options are accessible via the **Wrap Settings** dialog, which includes these useful illustrations of how text flows in each instance:

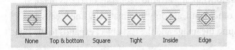

To wrap text around an object:

1. Select the object around which you want the text to wrap.

2. Click the ⬚ **Wrap Settings** button on the Arrange toolbar, or choose **Wrap Settings...** from the Arrange menu.

The **Wrap Settings** dialog lets you select the manner in which text will wrap around the object. For example, with **Tight** wrapping, text wraps closely around the object's contours.

In addition, you can specify the **Distance from text**: the "standoff" between the object's **wrap outline** and adjacent text. (The wrap outline is a contour that defines the object's edges for text wrapping purposes.) Different object types have different initial wrap outlines. For QuickShapes the wrap outline corresponds exactly to the object's edges, while for closed shapes the outline is a rectangle.

You can manually adjust the wrap outline using the Curve context toolbar for more precise text fitting. See PagePlus Help for more information.

Flowing text around inline images

An "inline" image is one you've **imported** at an insertion point in a text object, or have pasted into a text object. (Where text flow is concerned, inline picture frames behave just like inline images.) Both **frame** and **artistic** text will flow around an inline image if the picture's alignment setting is Left, Centre, Right, or Indent, but not if it's Top, Middle, or Bottom. You can also adjust the Distance from text, which (as with regular text wrap) affects the "standoff" between the object and adjacent text. In the illustration at right below, the standoff is .5 cm all round.

With frame text, the effect is similar to wrapping around a separate object, as detailed above. Lines of artistic text, on the other hand, are only terminated by line breaks and don't wrap—rather they break around the image and the text object expands to the right.

To flow text around an inline image or picture frame:

1. Right-click it and choose **Properties...**.

2. Set the **Align** option to **Left**, **Centre**, **Right**, or **Indent**.

    Note: You can also right-click an inline image and choose **Align**, then select an option from the submenu.

3. In the **Picture Properties** dialog, set the indent amount (if any) and the **Distance from text**, then click **OK**.

> You can also adjust the indent amount by dragging the picture left or right.

Creating a bulleted, numbered, or multi-level list

You can turn a series of paragraphs into **bulleted**, **numbered** or **multi-level lists**. Bullets are especially useful when listing items of interest in no specific order of preference, numbered lists for presenting step-by-step procedures (by number or letter), and multi-level lists for more intelligent hierarchical lists with prefixed numbers, symbols, or a mix of both, all with supporting optional text (see **Using Multi-level lists** on p. 100).

Bulleted list   Numbered list   Multi-level list

PagePlus lets you choose from a selection of preset bullet, number or multi-level styles and apply the list style to normal text (as local formatting) or to **text styles** equally. If you want to go a step further you can create custom list styles by selecting your own symbols, numbers and letter formats. You then have the option of replacing an existing preset with your own preset based on your custom list style.

To create a bulleted or numbered list:

1. Select one or more paragraphs.
    OR
    Click in a paragraph's text.

2. Select **Bullets & Numbering...** from the Format menu.

3. From the Text Style dialog, choose **Bullet**, **Number**, or **Multi-Level** from the drop-down menu.

4. Select one of the preset formats shown by default.
    OR
    For a custom list, click the **Details** button to display then alter custom options.

5. Click **OK** to apply list formatting.

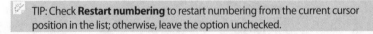

TIP: Check **Restart numbering** to restart numbering from the current cursor position in the list; otherwise, leave the option unchecked.

Each time you insert a following return, a new line will begin with the specified symbol or number. In addition, typing two returns in a row (pressing **Enter** twice) cancels bullets or numbers and resumes regular paragraph formatting.

To restart list numbering:

1. Click an item in the list to set the restart position, then select **Bullets & Numbering...** from the Format menu.

2. From the Presets or Details page, check **Restart Numbering** to reset the number or letter sequence back to 1 or A, respectively.

3. Click **OK**.

To turn off bullets, numbering or multi-level list formatting:

1. Select the paragraph with list formatting.

2. Select **Bullets & Numbering...** from the Format menu.
    OR
    Right-click the paragraph and from the **Text Format** option, choose **Bullets & Numbering...**.

3. In the **Text Styles** dialog, click the **None** preset option.

Using Multi-level lists

For multi-level lists, as opposed to bulleted and numbered lists, you can set a different character (symbol, text or number) to display at each level of your list. Levels are normally considered to be subordinate to each other, where Level 1 (first level), Level 2 (second), Level 3 (third), etc. are of decreasing importance in the list. For example, the following simple multi-level numbered passage of text is arranged at three levels.

1   Vestibulum velit orci
         Nullam sed enim. Du
  1.1   Lorem ipsum
            pendisse poter
  1.2   Mauris vitae a
            nean arcu elit,
            ligula.
      1.2.1   Quisqu
      1.2.2   Donec
               Duis b
               molest
               tum le

2   In hac habitasse plate
         Proin mattis eleifend

3   Proin mattis eleifend
         pede tellus, dictum eg

The flexibility of PagePlus's multi-level bullet and numbering system means that you have full control over what gets displayed at each level. For this reason, no hierarchy needs to exist between levels, i.e. the list could equally be prefixed with a different symbol, text prefix, or number combination at each level.

If you apply a multi-level preset to a range of text you'll get a list with the preset's Level 1 format applied by default. Unless you use **text styles**, you'll have to change to levels 2, 3, 4, etc. to set the correct level for your list entry.

Changing list levels on selected paragraphs:

- Click the **Increase Level** button on the Text context toolbar to increment the current level by one. The **Decrease Level** button does the opposite.

The multi-level presets offer some simple but commonly used schemas for paragraph list formatting. However, if you want to create your own lists or modify an existing list, PagePlus lets you create your own preset (or modify an existing one).

Creating a multi-level list from selected paragraphs:

1. Select **Bullets & Numbering...** from the Format menu.

2. With the **Style** drop-down menu set to Multi-level, select the list preset called **None**, and click the **Details** button.

3. From the dialog, you can use the **Format** field to build up a list format for the currently selected **Level**. Pick the Level then the **List type**, which could be bulleted, numeric, roman numeric, or alphabetic.

4. Choose a **Start at** value from which the currently set level's sequence will begin.

5. Adjust the character position details including indents (**Number at** and **Text indent**), first tab position (**Tabstop at**), and list **Align** for that level.

6. Repeat the process for each subsequent level needed for the list. You can edit the **Format** structure for each new level if needed.

To modify an existing preset, select it from the list and click the **Details** button. Change the list settings as described above and select the **OK** button.

When you create any type of list, whether bulleted, numbered or multi-level, the list's settings can be recalled by reselecting any part of the list and choosing **Bullets & Numbering...** from the Format menu. If a preset was used, PagePlus remembers this and shows the presets page; if the list was a custom list (and not saved as a preset) the Details page is shown. It's possible to save the custom list as a preset at any time.

To save list as new preset:

1. Click anywhere on a custom list, then select **Bullets & Numbering...** from the Format menu to display the Details page.

2. Click the **Preset** button, then pick a preset that you want to overwrite.

3. A dialog prompts you to overwrite the preset, i.e. "*Store current list in preset n?*." Select **Yes** to overwrite the existing preset.

Assigning bullets or numbers to styles

The lists discussed so far are usually applied as local formatting to a single style, typically "Normal" or "Body Text". To prove this, you'll see the list structure disappear if you apply **Clear Formatting** (from the Text Styles tab) on the selected list.

If you're working on long documents, there's a fair chance that you're using pre-assigned **text styles** (Heading 1, Heading 2, indent, etc.) to format your document rather than using the above local formatting. You can use such text styles along with list styles to number headings or paragraphs automatically without the need to repetitively format headings or paragraphs as lists. As an example, headings and paragraphs in technical and legal documents are typically prefixed by numbers for easy reference. The advantage of using a style-driven approach is that your can let the numbering take care of itself while you concentrate on applying styling to your document.

PagePlus lets you easily associate any bulleted, numbered or multi-level list style (either preset or custom list) to an existing text style. See **Using text styles** on p. 90.

Inserting a symbol

You can insert any character from any font installed on your system, using either the Insert menu or (for common symbols) keyboard shortcuts. You can also use a convenient keyboard switch to enter **subscripts** or **superscripts**.

To insert a symbol character using the Insert menu:

1. Select the Pointer Tool and click in the text for an insertion point.

2. Choose **Symbol...** from the Insert menu, and select a symbol from the submenu.

3.   If you need a symbol not shown on the submenu, select **Other** to display the
     Insert Symbol dialog. The dialog remains open so you can continue editing in
     the workspace as you select symbols.

     • Select a **Font** to display its full character set, and then scroll the font table to
     view characters. You can choose from the **Subset** list to jump to a particular
     range within the character set.

     • Click any individual character (or select it while browsing using the arrow
     keys on your keyboard) to view the character's name and Unicode Index at the
     bottom of the dialog. You can also enter any Unicode hex value and click **Go**
     to jump to that particular character in the current font.

     • To insert a character into your text, double-click it (or select it and click
     Insert).

To enter subscript or superscript characters:

●   Press **Ctrl**+= to enter subscript mode, or **Ctrl+Shift**+= to for superscript mode.
    Type the subscript or superscript, then press the key combination again to return to
    entering regular characters.

Inserting date/time

You can insert a date/time field into your text, stamped with current date/time
information, by using **Information>Date or Time...** from the Insert menu. Various
date and time formats are available. By default, the date/time field updates itself
automatically when the publication is saved or loaded. You can turn auto-updating off if
necessary.

Inserting user details

When you **create a publication using a Design Template** for the first time, you may be
prompted to update your user details (from a User Details dialog) which will then be
used for subsequent design templates. This means you don't need to re-enter the same
information the next time it's required in your next Design Template. (Note that some
templates don't make use of these user details so a prompt may not occur.)

You can also use this User Details dialog to review your User Details at any time.

Whether opening a template, or updating an existing publication, the fields (once
edited) can be updated at the click of a button.

To switch off prompting for user details, uncheck the **Show when opening new templates** check box in the User Details dialog.

To add, edit or change User Details:

1. Choose **Set User Details...** from the Tools menu.

2. Enter new information into the spaces on the **Business**, **Home**, or **Custom** tab (a **Calendars** tab will appear if there is a calendar in your publication).

You can also insert one or more User Details fields into any publication at any time. The **Custom** tab of the User Details dialog includes modifiable and nameable fields into which you can enter any information you may frequently need to "plug into" your publications.

To insert a User Detail field:

1. Select the Pointer Tool and click in the text for an insertion point.

2. Choose **Information** from the Insert menu, then select **User Details...** from the submenu.

3. Select a User Detail entry, and optionally any text **Prefix** or suffix (**Postfix**) to include with your user details, e.g. *Name:*.

4. Click **OK**.

To update fields:

- Enter new information in the User Details dialog (via **Tools>Set User Details**).

- Click the **Update** button to automatically update any altered field currently placed in your publication or template. This field will remain linked to User Details until it is deleted.

Viewing and changing document information

PagePlus maintains basic properties and statistics for each publication file.

To view or change document properties:

1. Choose **Properties...** from the File menu.

2. Click the **Summary** tab to view or change fields for Title, Subject, Author, Keywords, and Comments.

3. Click the **Statistics** tab to view key dates, last saved information, etc.

To insert document information in your text:

1. Select the Pointer Tool and click in the text for an insertion point.

2. Choose **Information** from the Insert menu, then select **Publication Info...** from the submenu. Select a property to insert and click **OK**.

If the document information changes and **Update automatically** is checked, the document information field in the text is automatically updated when the publication is saved or loaded.

Using AutoCorrect and AutoSpell

PagePlus includes two powerful support tools to nip possible spelling errors in the bud. The **AutoCorrect** feature overcomes common typing errors and lets you build a custom list of letter combinations and substitutions to be applied automatically as you type. You can also turn on the **AutoSpell** feature to mark possible problem words in your story text in red. Both features apply to frame text, table text, and artistic text.

If you prefer to address spelling issues in larger doses, at any point along the way you can run the **Spell Checker**.

AutoCorrect

To set options for automatic text correction:

1. Choose **Options...** from the Tools menu and select the **Auto-Correct** page.

2. Check your desired correction options as required.
   Note: Check **Replace text while typing** to turn on AutoCorrect.

To create a correction list:

1. In the **Replace** field, type a name for the AutoCorrect entry. This is the abbreviation or word to be replaced automatically as you type. For example, if you frequently mistype "product" as "prodcut," type "prodcut" in the Replace box.

2. In the **With** field, type the text to be automatically inserted in place of the abbreviation or word in the **Replace** field.

3. Click the **Add** button to add the new entry to the list.

4. To modify an entry in the correction list, select it in the list, then edit it in the **Replace** and **With** field above. Click the **Replace** button below.

5. To remove an entry, select it and click **Delete**.

To turn off AutoCorrect:

- Uncheck Replace text while typing.

AutoSpell

To turn AutoSpell on (or off):

1. Choose **Options...** from the Tools menu.

2. On the General tab, check (or uncheck) **Autospell**.

When AutoSpell is activated, possible problem words in your story text are marked in red, and you can view a list of suggested alternatives.

To view alternatives:

1. Right-click a marked word.

2. To replace a marked word, choose an alternative spelling from the menu.

3. To tell PagePlus to ignore (leave unmarked) all instances of the marked word in the publication, choose **Ignore All** from the right-click menu.

4. To add the marked word (as spelled) to your personal dictionary, choose **Add to Dictionary** from the right-click menu. This means PagePlus will subsequently ignore the word in any publication.

5. To run the Spelling Checker Wizard, choose **Check Spelling...** from the menu.

Spell-checking

The **Spell Checker** lets you check the spelling of a single word, selected text, a single story, or all text in your publication. (To help trap spelling errors as they occur, use the PagePlus **AutoCorrect** and **AutoSpell** features.) You can customize the built-in dictionary by adding your own words (see PagePlus help).

Multilingual spell checking is supported by use of up to 14 dictionaries. Any language can be enabled globally from **Tools>Options>General tab** or applied specifically to text or paragraphs via the Language Selector in the Character tab. Spell checking can be turned off temporarily by selecting "None" as a language type—this could be useful when working with text containing lots of unusual terms (perhaps scientific or proprietary terminology).

To check spelling:

1. (Optional) To check a single story, first make sure the text or text object is selected.

2. Choose **Spell Checker...** from the Tools menu.
   OR
   (In WritePlus) Click the ▣ **Spell Check** button.

3. In the dialog, click **Options...** to set preferences for ignoring words in certain categories, such as words containing numbers or domain names.

4. Select **Check currently selected story only** or **Check all stories in my publication** to select the scope of the search.

5. Click **Start** to begin the spelling check.

When a problem is found, PagePlus highlights the problem word. The dialog offers alternative suggestions, and you can choose to **Change** or **Ignore** this instance (or all instances) of the problem word, with the option of adding the problem word to your dictionary. (See below for more on modifying your dictionary.)

6. Spell checking continues until you click the **Close** button or the spell-check is completed.

To check the spelling of a single word:

1. With the AutoSpell feature turned on, select in a marked word, then right-click. You'll see alternative spellings on the context menu.

2. To replace the word, choose an alternative spelling from the menu.

3. To tell PagePlus to ignore (leave unmarked) all instances of the marked word in the publication, choose **Ignore All**.

4. To add the marked word (as spelled) to your personal dictionary, choose **Add to Dictionary**. This means PagePlus will ignore the word in any publication.

5. To run the Spell Checker, choose **Check Spelling...**.

Automatic proofreading

The **Proof Reader** checks for grammar and readability errors in selected text, a single story, or all text in your publication. You can use Proof Reader from either PagePlus or WritePlus.

To start automatic proofreading:

1.   To check a single story, first make sure the text or text object is selected.

2.   Choose **Proof Reader...** from the Tools menu.

3.   If necessary, click the **Options** button to set options for proofreading, including a spell-check option and the level of formality (with checks for rule types).

4.   Select **Check currently selected story only** or **Check all stories in my publication** to select the scope of the search.

5.   Click **Start** to begin proof reading.

When a problem is found, PagePlus highlights the problem word. The dialog offers alternative suggestions, and you can choose to **Change** or **Ignore** this instance (or all instances) of the problem word.

6.   Proofreading continues until you click the **Close** button or the process is completed.

Using the thesaurus

The **Thesaurus** lets you find synonyms, definitions, and variations of words in text objects throughout the publication. You can use the Thesaurus from either PagePlus or WritePlus.

To display the Thesaurus:

1.   To look up a specific word, first drag to highlight it.

2.   Choose **Thesaurus...** from the Tools menu or press **Shift+F7**.

3.   To look up a different word, type it into the "Replace/Look Up" box and click the **Look Up** button.

Using the Thesaurus

If the word entered is found in the thesaurus database:

- The "Meanings" list shows definitions for the word in the "Looked Up" box. Initially, the first definition is selected.

- The "Synonyms" list shows synonyms for the definition selected in the "Meanings" box. Initially, the first synonym appears in the "Replace/Look Up" box.

To pop a new word into the "Replace/Look Up" box:

- Click the word in the "Synonyms" list.
  OR

  Type a new word directly into the "Replace/Look Up" box.

You can navigate indefinitely through the thesaurus by selecting the specific meaning, followed by the specific synonym you are interested in and then clicking on the **Look Up** button to get a new range of meanings and synonyms for the new word.

To replace the original word:

- Click the **Replace** button to replace the original word (selected in your text) with the word in the "Replace/Look Up" box.

To exit the thesaurus:

- Click the **Cancel** button.

Creating text-based tables

Tables are ideal for presenting text and data in a variety of easily customizable row-and-column formats, with built-in spreadsheet capabilities.

10	*Tagetes*	44X-123
22	*Viola*	12Z-222
5	*Tropaeolum maju*	89X-XX2
13	*Pelargonium*	34W-6YY

Each cell in a table behaves like a mini-frame. There are many similarities (and several key differences) between **frame text** and table text.

- With table text, you can vary **character and paragraph properties**, apply named **text styles**, embed **inline images**, track font usage with the **Resource Manager**, and use proofing options such as **AutoSpell/Spell Checker**, **Proof Reader**, and **Thesaurus**.

- However, tables don't support importing text from a file, editing text with WritePlus or viewing it with the Text Manager, or wrapping text around objects. And table text doesn't flow or link the way frame text does; the Frame context toolbar's text-fitting functions aren't applicable.

- Tables also have a number of unique features like **AutoFormat**, **QuickClear and QuickFill** for rapid editing and revision.

- Filter effects can be applied to all of your table text simultaneously—apply **shadows, glow, bevel, emboss, and colour fills**. Note that filter effects cannot be applied on a per cell basis.

- Microsoft Excel spreadsheet contents can be pasted directly onto a selected cells within your PagePlus table.

To create a table:

1. On the Tools toolbar, choose the ▦ **Table Tool** from the Table flyout and click on the page or pasteboard, or drag to set the table's dimensions. The **Create Table** dialog opens with a selection of preset layouts.

2. Step through the list to preview the layouts and select one. To begin with a plain table, select **Default**.

3. Click **OK** to display the new table on the page.

Manipulating tables

Once you've created a table, you can select, move, resize, delete, and copy the table object and its contents, just as you can with a text frame. **Cell properties** can also be modified.

To manipulate the table object:

- To select the table object, click its bounding box. Now you can resize it like a text frame by dragging a node, or move it by dragging an edge.

- To delete the table object, select it and press the **Delete** key, or select any part of its text and choose **Delete** from the Table menu (**Table/Delete** from the right-click menu), then **Table** (or **All**) from the submenu. You can also choose **Delete Object** from the Edit menu.

- To duplicate the selected table object and its text, first make sure no text is selected (an insertion point is OK), then use the **Copy** and **Paste** commands. As a shortcut, select the object and drag with the **Ctrl** key pressed down.

To select and edit text in cells, rows, and columns:

- To select a cell, click for an insertion point or drag to select text. To select more than one cell, click in one cell and drag across the others, one row or column at a time.

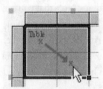

- To move to the next or previous cells, use the **Tab** or **Shift+Tab** key, respectively, or the keyboard arrow keys.

- To enter text, simply type into a cell at the insertion point. Cells expand vertically as you type to accommodate extra lines of text. To enter a Tab character, press **Ctrl+Tab**.

- To select a row or column, click its control button along the left or top of the table. To select more than one row or column, drag across their control buttons.

- To select all text (all rows and columns), choose **Select** from the Table menu.

- To copy, paste and delete selected table text, use the **Copy**, **Paste** and **Delete** commands as you would for frame text. Alternatively, drag the bottom corner of a selected cell to copy its table text to any of the newly selected cells. Drag and drop support between cells lets you replicate text to other cells—for more power, use **Shift**-drag to replicate all text and cell formatting to other cells simultaneously. Copy and paste of Microsoft Excel spreadsheet cells into PagePlus and HTML tables is also possible.

- To format selected text, apply **character and paragraph properties** or **text styles** as with any text.

- To rotate selected text, right-click and choose **Table>Cell Properties**. In the **Orientation** tab, use the rotation dial to set a rotation angle or enter a specific value into the input box.

- Table text shares default properties with frame text. For details, see **Default text properties** on p . 84.

- Table text can be sorted by row, column, multi-row, multi-column regions or entire table. For details, see **Sorting tables** on p . 113.

To change the table's structure and appearance:

- To adjust row or column size, drag the ↔ control button shown when hovering over the separating lines in the table row or column headings. Note that you can adjust a row's height independent of the amount of text it contains. For absolute row/column sizing, choose **Set column width(s)** or **Set row height(s)** from the Table menu (or use the right-click menu). You can resize your columns without affecting the overall table width by adjusting the column heading with **Ctrl**-drag.

- To distribute rows or columns, select the entire table or just a selection of rows or columns, then choose **Evenly Distribute Rows** or **Evenly Distribute Columns** from the Table menu (or use the right-click menu). To honour table width, a cell's text may wrap when distributing columns.

- Choose **Autofit Column(s) to contents** from the Table menu (or right-click menu) to reduce or increase the size of selected columns to fit to the text of the greatest width. An equivalent option exists for rows.

- To delete one or more rows or columns, select them (or cell text), then choose **Delete** from the Table menu (**Table>Delete** from the right-click menu), then either **Row(s)** or **Column(s)** from the submenu.

- To insert new rows or columns, select one or more cells as described above, then choose **Insert** from the Table menu (**Table>Insert** from the right-click menu), then either **Rows...** or **Columns...** from the submenu. In the dialog, specify how many to add, and whether to add them before or after the selected cells.

- To merge cells into larger cells that span more than one row or column (for example, a column head), select a range of cells and choose **Merge Cells** from the Table menu (**Table>Merge Cells** from the right-click menu). The merged cell displays only the text originally visible in the top left selected cell. The original cells and their text are preserved, however—to restore them, select the merged cell and choose **Separate Cells** from the Table menu (**Table>Separate Cells** from the right-click menu).

- To copy cell contents (including text, formatting, borders, and colours) to a new cell in the same table, select the cell(s), press the **Ctrl** key and hover over the cell border(s) until the copy cursor is shown—click and drag the copied cell to its new cell location. To copy cell contents from one table to another table select the cells, right-click on a cell selection and choose **Copy**—select the area (of the same dimension) in the new table then select **Paste**.

- To move cell contents within the same table, select the cells, and when the cursor is displayed, drag the cell(s) to the new location.

Using AutoFormat

To use style presets to customize the table's appearance:

- Choose **AutoFormat...** from the Table menu. The dialog presents a list of sample tables, which differ in their use of **Lines** (inner and outer cell borders), **Fill** (cell fill), **Font** (bold, italic, etc.), and **Alignment** (left, centre, etc.).

- You can pick any sample and use the check boxes to specify which of the sample's attribute(s) to apply to your actual table. This lets you "mix and match," for example by applying (in two passes) the Colour from one sample and the Font from another.

- To restore plain formatting, choose **Default**.

Setting Cell Properties

To customize the appearance of one or more cells "by hand":

1. Select the cell(s) and choose **Cell Properties...** from the Table menu.

2. Use the dialog's **Border**, **Fill**, **Transparency**, **Margin**, or **Orientation** tabs to apply cell formatting, then click **OK**.

Sorting tables

PagePlus lets you sort words, numbers or a combination of both in a single row or column, any selected table area or the entire table. Sorting can be carried out in ascending (A to Z, or 0 to 9) or descending order (Z to A, or 9 to 0) to a set priority: punctuation marks first, then numbers, letters, and symbols last.

More complex multi-row or multi-column sorting is possible—especially useful when sorting first names and surnames. Typically you'd want to order by surname but for

people with identical surnames (e.g., Walker) you may also want to additionally order
their first names (Andrew, Kate, and Paul).

Sort by
columns:

First By
Column B,
then by
Column A

A key point in table sorting is the issue of **dependencies**. This means the linkage of
"connected" data contained within one cell and another which, when broken, destroys
the value of the information stored (think of a person's first name becoming
disconnected from his/her last name by sorting). To avoid breaking such dependencies,
you have to select the whole table rather than just selecting a table region or
row/column.

 Take care not to break dependencies by sorting specific regions, rows or
columns within your table (especially on more complex database tables)!

To sort a table:

1. Select the table in which you want to sort data.

2. Select the ⬇️ **Sort** button from the context toolbar.
    OR
    Select **Sort** from the Table menu.
    OR
    Right-click on the selected range and choose **Table>Sort...**.

3. In the dialog's Order tab, choose to sort **Rows** or **Columns** from the **Sort by**
    drop-down menu.

4. Three drop-down menus (First by, Then by, Then by) let you set the first
    row/column to be sorted, a subsequent row/column (for identical first
    row/column data), then a final row/column (for identical second row/column
    data) in either **Ascending** or **Descending** order.

5. Enable the **A header** button if you've used named headers above or preceding your row or column. Specify the named row or column headers from the above drop-down menus to ignore the headers during the sorting process.

6. Swap to the Options tab, and pick the **Primary sort key order**. Keep the setting at **Normal** unless your list contains weekdays or months, in which case pick a date format from the same drop-down menu (this must match your list's date format). This will then sort on month order rather than alphabetic order.

7. Check **Case Sensitive** to separate out lower case characters from upper case characters (which list first).

8. To check **Treat numbers as text** to order number lists as 1, 10, 12, 3, 5 instead of 1, 3, 5, 10, 12.

Using QuickClear and QuickFill

QuickClear and **QuickFill** are handy shortcuts built into tables. Both employ the small "QuickFill handle" which you may have noticed at the lower right of each selected cell (or range of cells).

QuickClear lets you instantly clear a range of cells whereas **QuickFill** lets you quickly enter a standard sequence of numbers or entries, for example the months of the year, the days of the week, or any arithmetic progression (see below). You can also use QuickFill to replicate one cell's contents over a range of cells.

To QuickClear a range of cells:

1. Select the range to be cleared.

2. Drag the QuickFill handle upward until no cells are specified.

To QuickFill a sequence of entries:

1. Type the first entry of the sequence into the starting cell.

2. Drag the selected cell's QuickFill handle out to the range of cells to be quick filled, as shown below. The function works both backwards and forwards!

If there are not enough items in the QuickFill sequence, the entries wrap back to the beginning value in the sequence.

To replicate a cell's contents over a range of cells:

1. Click to select the cell whose contents you want to replicate.

2. Drag out the cell's QuickFill handle over the range you want to fill.

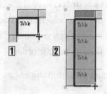

For **numerical sequences**, if the starting selection contains two or more cells, QuickFill uses the difference between them as the common difference. For example, if the first two cells contain the numbers 10 and 20, then the 'quick filled' sequence would be: 10, 20, 30, ... If only a single number is specified, then the common difference between the numbers will be 1.

Similarly, for **non-numerical sequences**, you can specify a step between any entries, for example, enter "January" in the first cell, "March" in the second. QuickFill will place every other month in the sequence: "January, March, May, July, ..."

You can type also phrases including **known sequences**, and QuickFill will fill the sequence, along with the other words. For example, type "Week 1" and QuickFill would give you the sequence "Week 1, Week 2, Week 3, ..." or "Jan Sales" would give: "Jan Sales, Feb Sales, Mar Sales, ..."

Formatting numbers

The Table context toolbar includes additional buttons, switched on with the $^{A}_{B}$
Spreadsheet functions button, that let you vary how numbers are displayed. Number formats let you add commas and currency signs to numbers, express numbers as percents, control how many decimal places are displayed, etc. Number formats <u>do not</u> alter numbers internally—only the way numbers are displayed.

See PagePlus help for more information.

Inserting formulas

A table cell can display the result of a **formula** combining values of other cells with arithmetic operators and functions. Formulas are recalculated whenever values in the table change, so they're always up to date.

Any cell starting with the character "=" is treated as a formula. To enter or edit formulas, use the Table context toolbar's edit field. Note that you can only select or edit an entire formula, not just part of it.

 Remember to enable the **Spreadsheet functions** button (on the Table context toolbar) to allow you to create formulas.

To display a cell's formula for editing in the Table context toolbar's edit field:

- Click to select the cell containing the formula.

To enter a formula:

- Click the 𝑓· **Function** button on the Table context bar and choose a specific function from the drop-down menu.
  For example, if you start with a blank cell and choose **SUM()**, PagePlus adds "=SUM()" to the edit field and positions the text cursor between the brackets so that you can type numbers or cell references straight away.
  OR

- Click the **Function** button once to seed the edit field with an equal sign (or type "=" yourself), then continue to type the formula.

Click the ✔ **Accept** button to update the selected cell.

See the PagePlus Help for a more detailed explanation of operators, percentages, values and functions used in formulas.

Inserting a calendar

The **Calendar Wizard** helps you design month-at-a-glance calendars for use in your publication.

The calendar is created as a scalable **text-based table** so you can edit text using the standard text tools. The properties of a selected calendar are similar to those of a table—a context toolbar lets you change text formatting, cell formatting, and from an **Edit Calendar** button, modify calendar-specific properties.

The wizard also sets up your country's public holidays while the **Calendar Event Manager** lets you add personal events before or after adding a calendar to the page.

If you have adopted a calendar-based design template, you'll be initially prompted to configure **global** calendar details via a User Details dialog. This updates all calendar details throughout your PagePlus document—in the same way that you'd set up the date (along with the time) on some alarm clocks.

To insert a calendar:

1. Click the Table flyout on the Tools toolbar and choose ▦ **Insert Calendar**.

2. Click again on your page, or drag out to indicate the desired size of the calendar.

3. From the displayed **Calendar Wizard**, define options for your calendar including setting the year and month, calendar style (square, or in single or double column format), week start day, room to write, display options, switching on events/holidays, and calendar format.

   If you want to have your country's public holidays shown, remember to check the **Add public holidays** option in Calendar Properties and select a **Region** from the associated drop-down menu. Equally, personal events must be switched on via the **Add personal events** option.

4. Click the **Finish** button to complete the wizard.

To update a calendar template's user details

1. Open a calendar design template.

2. From the displayed **User Details** dialog, pick the **Year** that your calendar will adopt from the drop-down menu.

3. In the Events box, check the **Show public holidays** and/or **Show personal events** if your template's calendar(s) are to adopt those holidays or events already configured in the Calendar Event Manager (you can modify personal events by clicking the **Events** button).

If you plan to use your calendar in subsequent years, simply update the **Year** setting in **Tools>Set User Details** (use the dialog's Calendars tab if not shown).

To view and edit a selected calendar's properties:

1. Click the **Edit Calendar** button on the Calendar context toolbar.
   OR
   Right-click on a selected calendar, and choose **Calendar>Edit Calendar....**

2. Choose an appropriate tab and make your modification, then press **OK**.

Right-click (with the **Calendar** option selected) also lets you select, insert, distribute, and delete rows and columns, but take care not to corrupt your table formatting!

Adding public holidays

When you create a calendar you can set up the appropriate public holidays for the country you reside in.

The holidays will show up in your calendar automatically. You can also swap to a different country's public holiday settings for any existing calendar if needed.

 Remember to ensure that **Add public holidays** is checked in Calendar Properties.

To swap public holidays:

1. Select a calendar.

2. Select the **Edit Calendar** button from the context toolbar (then navigate to the Events tab).

3. Select a different name from the **Region** drop-down menu.

Adding personal events

You can complement your public holiday listings (e.g., Easter holidays) by adding personal events such as birthdays, anniversaries, and bill payments (unfortunately!) so that the events show up on your calendar—simply use the **Calendar Events** button on a selected calendar's context toolbar. Events show automatically on your calendar under the chosen date.

To add an event:

1. Select a calendar.

2. Choose **Calendar Events** from the context toolbar.
   OR
   Select the **Calendar Event Manager** from the Tools menu.

3. Check **Show events by date** to view your events in a more traditional calendar layout.

4. Ensure that **Show personal events** is enabled.

5. Click the 🖻 **New Event** button.

6. From the dialog, type, use the up/down arrows, or click the 🖾 **Browse** button to select a date.

7. Enter your event text into the text input box. This displays in your calendar under the chosen date.

8. If the event is a birthday or other annual event, check **Event recurs annually**.

9. Click the **OK** button. The event appears in the event list under the chosen date.

Click the **Save** button to finish adding events.

Use the 🖻 **Edit Event** or ✕ **Delete Event** buttons to modify or delete an existing event, respectively.

> Remember to ensure that **Add personal events** is checked in Calendar Properties.

Inserting database tables

As a great way of producing a database report in your publication, it is possible for a database table to be imported and presented as a PagePlus table. The database table could be from one of a comprehensive range of database file formats, as well as from HTML files and various delimited text files.

For a high degree of control, it is also possible to filter and sort your database records prior to import.

To insert a database table:

1. Click the **Table** flyout on the Tools toolbar and choose ▦ **Insert Database table** from the submenu.

2. Using the pointer, draw an area on your page that will contain your database information.

TIP: If there are many fields in your database table you may consider presenting the information on a page with landscape orientation. Alternatively, you can choose only a subset of those fields (see below).

3. In the **Open** dialog, select from the Files of Type drop-down menu the database file that contains the table you require.

4. Navigate to your database file and click **Open**.

5. The **Select Table** dialog displays the tables within your database. Select your table and click **OK**.

6. The **Merge List** dialog shows all the table rows (records) in the table—choose to **Select All** records, **Toggle Select** (invert all current selections) or use a custom **Filter...**

7. The list of fields available in the table are shown in the **Select Fields** dialog. Uncheck any fields that you don't want to be included in the import process. Again, Select All or Toggle selection options are available.

8. Click the **OK** button.

Filtering your records

Records can be filtered by using the Filter Records tab then subsequently sorted into any combination with the Sort Records tab. The Filter option helps you limit the number of records imported to only those you require.

For example, only records from people living in London with an interest in Ice hockey could be included for import, i.e.

Note that the Boolean operator "And" used to include both terms (as in this example). If the "Or" operator was used records from either London or Ice hockey would be included for import.

The Sort Records tab is used to sort by three prioritised field names, either in ascending or descending order.

Creating a table of contents

The Table of Contents Wizard helps you create a table of contents with headings up to six levels deep, derived from named styles in your publication. If you're exporting to PDF format, PagePlus can automatically build a **bookmark list** using the same style markings in your text.

To create a table of contents:

1. Decide which named styles you want to designate as headings at each of up to six levels.

2. Check your publication to make sure these styles are used consistently.

3. Review the choices you'll need to make when you run the Table of Contents Wizard.

4. From the Insert menu, choose **Table of Contents...** to run the Wizard.

5. You can easily modify the look of your table of contents, or run the Wizard again to update the information.

Using styles to prepare a table of contents

The Wizard will show you a list of all the style names used in your publication, and you will check boxes to include text of a given style as a heading at a particular level (1 through 6). For example, you could pull out all text using the "Heading" style as your first-level headings.

Entries in the resulting table of contents will appear in the order the text occurs in your publication.

When the table of contents is created, PagePlus formats it using built-in **text styles** intended specifically for table of contents preparation: "Contents-Title" and "Contents-1st" through "Contents-6th". You can easily change the look of your table of contents by changing the style definitions for these built-in "Contents" styles.

Changing the look of your table of contents:

You can update the built-in Contents styles as needed, as explained in **Using text styles**.

Creating an index

An **index** is a valuable reader aid in a longer document such as a report or manual. The Index Wizard helps you create an index with **main entries** and **subentries**, based on **index entry marks** you insert.

To mark index entries:

1. Select a text frame and then choose **Edit Story** from the Edit menu. The WritePlus window opens.

2. Select the text to be included in the index, or click where you want to insert the index entry (before the first word you want to mark).

3. Click the **Mark Index** button on the **Story** toolbar.

4. Use the **Mark Index Entry** dialog to insert or edit index entry marks.

> Index entry marks are invisible on the PagePlus screen and can only be added or edited in WritePlus.

If you selected a word or phrase in the story, it appears as the main entry in the dialog. You can use the entry as it is, or type new text for the main entry and sub-entry (if any).

You must include a main entry for each sub-entry. The dialog's scrolling list records entries and sub-entries alphabetically.

- To reuse an entry, click it in the list.

- For a standard index entry, leave the **Current page** box checked.

- To insert a cross-reference with the term(s) preceded by "See:", select **Cross-reference** (to include a word other than "See," simply replace it in the box).

- You can also specify a bold and/or italic page number format.

- Click **Mark** to insert the new entry mark or update a selected mark.

- To undo a mark entry, click the **Undo** button or press **Ctrl+Z**.

To build an index:

First mark the entries as described above. Then in PagePlus...

1. Review the choices you'll need to make before running the Index Wizard (see below).

2. Choose **Index...** from the Insert menu.

You can easily modify the look of your index, or run the Wizard again to update the information.

Changing the look of your index:

You can update the built-in Index styles (Index-Title, -Separator, -Main, and -Sub) as needed, as explained in **Using text styles** on p. 90. For example, indent the "Index-Sub" text slightly, and introduce some space above the "Index-Separator" text.

Producing a book with BookPlus

BookPlus is a management utility built into PagePlus that lets you produce a whole book from a set of separate PagePlus (*.PPP) publication files. Using BookPlus, you can arrange the chapter files in a specific order, systematically **renumber** pages, **synchronize** styles and other elements between all chapters, create a **Table of Contents and/or Index** for the whole book, and **output** the book via printing, PostScript®, or PDF. BookPlus can perform all these managerial tasks whether or not the original files are open! Your settings are saved as a compact BookPlus (*.PPB) book file, separate from the source publication files.

Working with books and chapters

A book consists of a set of PagePlus (*.PPP) publication files. Each publication file is
considered a chapter in the book. To create a new book, you'll need at least one
constituent chapter file. Be sure to define similar **page setup options** (such as
dimensions and facing page structure) for each chapter, as BookPlus will not override
these publication-level settings.

To create a new book:

● In PagePlus, on the File menu, choose **New** and then click **New Book...**.

BookPlus opens with an empty central region reserved for the **chapter list**.

To add a chapter to the chapter list:

1. In BookPlus, on the **Chapter** menu, click **Add...**.

2. In the dialog, select one or more PagePlus files to be added as chapters. (Use
   the **Ctrl** or **Shift** keys to select multiple files or a range of files.) Click **Open**.

The selected files appear in the chapter list.

 Once you've created a chapter list, you can add new chapters at any time, or
replace/remove chapters in the current list (see below).

To reorder chapters in the list:

● Drag a chapter file's name (in the Chapter column) to the desired position.

To open one or more chapter files for editing:

● Double-click a specific chapter name in the Chapter column.
  OR

● Select one or more chapter names and choose **Open** from the **Chapter** menu.

The selected file(s) open in PagePlus. In BookPlus, any open chapters are listed as
"Open" in the Status column.

To replace or remove a chapter file:

● Select its name in the list and choose **Replace...** or **Remove** from the **Chapter**
  menu.

The Remove command deletes the chapter from the list. The Replace command displays
a dialog that lets you select another file to be substituted into the same position in the list.

Replace is useful if a file has been moved or externally modified and you need to update the BookPlus listing. Neither command affects the original file. Only the chapter list is updated.

To save the current chapter list as a book file:

- Choose **Save** (or **Save As...**) from the BookPlus **File** menu.

 You can open saved book files from PagePlus using **File/Open...**. You can have more than one book file open at a time.

Numbering pages

BookPlus provides a variety of options for incrementing page numbers continuously from one chapter to another, through the whole book. Page numbers will only appear on pages or (more commonly) **master pages** where you've inserted **page number fields**. To "suppress" page numbers—for example, on a title page—simply don't include a page number field there.

BookPlus lets you change page number style choices you've made in the original file (using **Format/Page Number Format...** in PagePlus), and provides other options such as inserting a blank page when necessary to force new chapters to start on a right-hand page. You don't need to have the original files open to update page numbering.

To set page numbering options for the book:

1. Choose **Book Page Number Options...** from the BookPlus **File** menu.

2. In the dialog, select whether you want page numbers to **Continue from previous chapter**, **Continue on next odd page**, or **Continue on next even page**. Typically you'll want new chapters to start on odd (right-hand or "recto") pages.

3. Leave **Insert blank page when necessary** checked if you want to output an extra page at the end of a chapter where the next page number (if you've selected odd- or even-page continuation) would otherwise skip a page. Either way, BookPlus will number your pages correctly—but for correct imposition in **professional printing** it's usually best to insert the blank page. **Note:** You won't see the blank page inserted into your original file, only in the generated output.

4. Click **OK**. BookPlus immediately applies your settings to all chapters.

To set page numbering options for a chapter:

1. Select its name in the list and choose **Chapter Page Number Options...** from the **Chapter** menu.

The **Page Number Format** dialog displays current settings for numbering style and initial numbering.

2. To change the numbering style, make a selection in the Style section. For example, you might use lowercase Roman numerals for a preface.

3. To force page numbering to start at a certain value, uncheck **Continue from previous chapter** and type the starting value. For example, you might want to skip page numbering for introductory ("front") matter and begin numbering from "1" on the first page of main body text.

4. Click **OK**. BookPlus immediately applies your settings to the selected chapter. **Note:** These settings only apply to the selected chapter.

If you've reordered chapters or changed the chapter list in any way, you can quickly impose correct numbering on the current list again.

To update page numbering:

- Choose **Renumber Pages** from the BookPlus **File** menu.

Synchronizing chapters

Synchronizing means imposing consistent styles, palettes, and/or colour schemes throughout the book. This is accomplished by using one chapter (called the **style source**) as a model for the rest of the book. You define attributes in the style source chapter, and then select which attributes should be adjusted in other chapters to conform to the style source. For example, you could redefine the "Normal" text style in your style source chapter, then quickly propagate that change through the rest of the book. The Modified and Synchronized columns of the BookPlus chapter list let you keep track of recent file changes.

To set one chapter as the style source:

- Select its name in the chapter list and choose **Set Style Source** from the **Chapter** menu.

The current style source is identified in the Synchronized column of the chapter list.

To synchronize one or more chapters with the style source:

1. To update just certain chapters, make sure their names are selected in the chapter list.

2. Choose **Synchronize...** from the **File** menu.

3. In the dialog, select whether you want to update **All** or just **Selected** chapters. Check which attributes should be updated to conform to those defined in the style source file: **Text styles**, **Object styles**, **Colour scheme**, and/or **Colour palette**.

4. Click **OK**.

BookPlus imposes the specified changes and updates the Synchronized time in the chapter list for each selected file. If the file was altered in any way, the Modified time updates as well.

Synchronizing does not alter **footnote or endnote** numbering.

Building a Table of Contents or Index

From BookPlus, you can build a **Table of Contents** and/or **Index** that includes entries for the entire set of chapters. In each case, you'll need to begin by designating a specific chapter where the resulting pages should be added.

To create a table of contents or index for the book:

1. Complete basic preparatory steps as described in **Creating a table of contents** or **Creating an index** on p . 122 or p. 123, respectively.

2. In the chapter list, select the name of the chapter file where you want to add the table of contents or index.

3. Choose **Insert** from the **Chapter** menu and select **Table of Contents...** or **Index...** from the submenu.

BookPlus opens the chapter file if it's not already open, and the Wizard for the procedure you've selected appears.

4. Select **Yes** when the Wizard asks if you want to build a table of contents or index for the entire book. Continue clicking **Next>** and selecting choices in the Wizard.

Printing and PDF output

When you **print** or generate **PDF output** from BookPlus, you'll have the choice of printing the entire book or selected chapters.

To print the book or selected chapters:

1. To print just certain chapters, make sure their names are selected in the chapter list.

2. Choose **Print...** from the BookPlus File menu.

3. Under "Print Range" on the General tab, select **Entire book** to output all chapters, or **Selected chapters** to output just those you selected. You can also select the **Pages** option to output one or more specific page(s). Whichever option you've chosen, a drop-down list lets you export all sheets in the range, or just odd or even sheets.

   Note: If you select **Print to file** to output **PostScript**, BookPlus will generate a separate file for each chapter.

4. Set other options as detailed in **Printing basics** (p. 193), then click **Print**.

To export the book or selected chapters as PDF:

1. To export just certain chapters, make sure their names are selected in the chapter list.

2. Choose **Publish as PDF...** from the BookPlus File menu.

3. Under "Print Range" on the General tab, select **Entire book** to output all chapters, or **Selected chapters** to output just those you selected. You can also select the **Pages** option to output one or more specific page(s). Whichever option you've chosen, a drop-down list lets you export all pages in the range, or just odd or even pages.

4. Set other options as detailed in **Exporting PDF files** on p. 201, then click **OK**.

Using mail merge

Most commonly, **mail merge** means printing your publication a number of times, inserting different information each time from a **data source** such as an address list file—for example into a series of form letters or mailing labels. PagePlus can handle many kinds of data sources and more challenging creative tasks. It is even possible to merge picture data (for example, digital photos) into single fields or even auto-create a grid layout of pictures and text suitable for catalogs or photo albums.

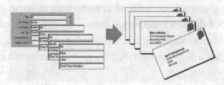

As mail merge is an advanced feature of PagePlus, see the PagePlus Help which covers mail merge in more detail. Subjects covered include:

- Opening a data source

- Editing Serif Database files

- Selecting, filtering, and sorting the merge list

- Inserting placeholders for your data

- Previewing data in the publication

- Merging and printing

Checking fonts and resources used

The **Resource Manager** lists the fonts and resources used in your publication, and shows if the pictures are linked to external picture files or embedded within the document. In addition, it will allow font substitution after import of PDF or opening of PagePlus files; this is necessary when fonts used in the publications are not available on your PC.

To display the Resource Manager:

- Choose **Resource Manager...** from the Tools menu.

Resources tab

The Resources tab lists imported pictures, media, Java applets, etc and their current status. It shows whether each is linked or embedded and lets you switch a resource from one mode to the other. "Linked" data consists of a reference to the original file. If you copy or move a publication with linked resources, for example from one computer to another, you should also copy any resource files linked to the publication.

To display the path name for a resource:

- Click on the resource name.

- The path appears below the Resources section.

To view a particular item:

- Double-click its name in the list.
  OR
  Select the item's name and click **Display**.

To switch an item from linked to embedded:

1. Select the item's name.

2. Click **Embed** to embed a linked item.

Conversely, click **Make Linked** to link an embedded item.

To check whether pictures you import are to be linked or embedded:

- Choose **Options...** from the Tools menu and click the **General** tab.

- Check **Suggest embed/link picture** for embedding or linking. Set a file size below which files are embedded automatically.

Fonts tab

The Fonts tab lists fonts used in text objects on individual pages or throughout the whole publication, along with their current status. The status column can display "OK" or "Missing". If "Missing" is shown then the font is not available on your PC. For this reason, if you are copying a publication to take to a different computer, you should check that the fonts used are available on the new computer.

A third column called Substitutions shows which local fonts are being used as substitutes for missing fonts. See **Substituting fonts** on p. 88 for more information.

To display the font category:

● Click on the font name.

The font category (TrueType, Printer, or System) appears below the Fonts section.

To view a particular item:

● Double-click its name in the list.
  OR
  Select the item's name and click **Display**.

Working with Images, Lines, and Shapes

Importing pictures

PagePlus lets you insert pictures from a wide variety of file formats, including bitmaps, vector images, and metafiles, and in several different ways. Here's a quick overview:

- **Bitmapped pictures**, also known as **bitmaps** or **raster pictures**, are built from a matrix of dots ("pixels"), rather like the squares on a sheet of graph paper. They may originate as digital camera photos or scanned pictures, or be created (or enhanced) with a "paint" program or photo editor.

- **Draw** graphics, also known as **vector images**, are resolution-independent and contain drawing commands such as "draw a line from A to B.".

- **Metafiles** are the native graphics format for Windows and combine raster and vector information.

You can also acquire pictures directly from PhotoCDs or via TWAIN devices (scanners or digital cameras)—see PagePlus help.

Inserting pictures

There are several ways to bring a picture into PagePlus. You can drag a file from an external Windows folder directly onto your page, drag a thumbnail from PagePlus's Media bar, or import a picture as an embedded or linked image via a dialog.. even place it into a picture frame.

- **Detached** pictures float freely on a page, while **inline** images are incorporated with the text flow in a text object.

- **Embedded** pictures become part of the publication file, while **linking** places a reference copy of the picture on the page and preserves a connection to the original file. Each approach has its pros and cons (see **Embedding vs. Linking** on p. 137).

- ⊠ **Picture frames** let you add your picture into a previously applied shaped frame. Choose from elliptical, star, heart, and triangular frames, amongst many others.

To import a picture from a file:

1. To place the picture inline, click for an insertion point in a text object.

    For a detached picture, make sure all text objects are deselected.

    To put the picture into a frame, create the frame and then select it.

2. <u>In the main window:</u>
    Click the ▨ **Import Picture...** button on the Tools toolbar's Picture flyout.

    <u>In WritePlus:</u>

    Choose **Picture File...** from the Insert menu.

1. Use the dialog to select the picture to open.

2. If you select the **Place at native dpi** option and the picture has a different internal setting, PagePlus will scale it accordingly; otherwise it applies a screen resolution setting of **96 dpi**. Either way—or if you resize it downwards later on—the picture retains all its original picture data until it's published.

3. Select either **Embed picture** or **Link picture** to include or exclude the picture from the project, respectively. Use linked pictures to minimize project file size.

4. Click **Open**.

5. If there's a text insertion point in the main window, you'll be prompted whether to insert the picture at the current cursor position. Click **Yes** if you want to do this.

    If there was no insertion point (or you answered **No** to the prompt), the mouse pointer changes to the ⁺▨ **Picture Paste** cursor. What you do next determines the initial size and placement of the detached picture.

6. To insert the picture at a default size, simply click the mouse.
    OR
    To set the size of the inserted picture, drag out a region and release the mouse button.

To replace an existing picture:

1. To replace an existing picture you can:

● Double-click it.
OR

Select it and click the ⬛ **Replace Picture** button on the Picture context toolbar.
OR
Right-click it and choose **Replace Picture...**.
OR
If the picture is in a picture frame, click the 🖼 button showing under the selected frame.

2. From the dialog, locate and select the replacement picture before clicking **Open**.

Embedding vs. linking

Embedding means the picture in PagePlus is now distinct from the original file. Embedding results in a larger PagePlus file, and if you need to alter an embedded picture you'll need to re-import it after editing. Still, it's the best choice if file size isn't an issue and graphics are final.

Linking inserts a copy of the picture file into the PagePlus publication, linked to the actual file so that any changes you later make to it in the native application will be automatically reflected in PagePlus. Linking is one way of avoiding "bloat" by limiting the size of the publication file. On the other hand, you'll need to manage the externally linked files carefully, for example making sure to include them all if you move the PagePlus file to a different drive.

By default, PagePlus prompts you to embed pictures that are smaller than 256 KB, by pre-selecting the "Embed Picture" option in the Insert Picture dialog (but you can always select "Link Picture" instead). If you like, you can change the threshold file size or even switch off the automatic selection.

You can use the **Resource Manager** later on, to change an item's status from linked to embedded, or vice versa.

To pre-select embedding or linking based on file size:

1. Choose **Options...** from the Tools menu. You'll see the **General** tab.

2. To pre-select the "Embed Picture" option for pictures under a certain size, select the threshold size in the "Embed if smaller than" list. ("Link Picture" will be pre-selected for pictures larger than the threshold.)

3. To choose whether to embed or link each picture, uncheck **Suggest embed/link picture**. You can still select either option in the import dialog; it will now remember and pre-select the last setting you used.

Adding picture frames

Not to be confused with a decorative **border**, a **picture frame** is a shaped container similar to a text frame. You can select any one of a series of shaped empty frames as a placeholder, and then import or drag a picture into it. At any time you can swap a different picture into the same frame. This gives you the flexibility of separating the container from its content—you can incorporate the picture frame into your layout irrespective of the actual picture that will go inside it.

You may encounter picture frames if you use photo-rich design templates such as those found in the Photo Album template category. When loaded, the picture frames display as blank placeholders ready for adding your own pictures (from the **Media Bar** or by using **Replace Picture**).

All picture frames, when selected, display a supporting Picture frame toolbar under the frame which offers panning, rotation (90 degrees anti-clockwise), zoom in, zoom out, and replace picture options (shown below from left to right).

Picture frames are always detached, i.e. they float freely on the page.

To add a picture to a frame:

1. For an empty square frame, choose **Picture>Empty Frame...** from the Insert menu.

   OR

   For a frame of a particular shape, e.g. **Elliptical Picture Frame**, choose a shape on the Import Picture flyout on the Tools toolbar.

2. ⬚ The mouse pointer changes to the **Picture Paste** cursor. What you do next determines the initial size and placement of the picture frame.

3. To insert the frame at a default size, simply click the mouse.

   OR

   To set the size of the frame, drag out a region and release the mouse button.

4. From the Media Bar's currently displayed album, drag and drop a photo directly onto the picture frame.

   OR

   Click the 🖉 **Replace Picture** button directly under the selected frame, locate and select an image. Click **Open**.

> Take advantage of the Gallery tab to drag and drop various bordered and basic picture frames onto your page. Choose from frames of different orientations and styles.

The picture is added to the frame using default Picture Frame properties, i.e. it is scaled to maximum fit. However, you can alter the picture's size, orientation and positioning relative to its frame; aspect ratio is always maintained.

To change picture size and positioning:

- Select a populated picture frame, and from the accompanying Picture frame toolbar:

  - Click the 🖐 button to position the photo in the picture frame by panning.

  - Click the 🖾 button to rotate the photo in 90 degree anti-clockwise increments.

  - Click the ⊕ ⊖ button to zoom in/out of the photo.

OR

1. Right-click on a picture frame and choose **Properties>Frame Properties....**
   OR
   Select the picture frame and choose **Frame Properties** on the Picture context toolbar.

2. In the dialog, you can scale to maximum/minimum, stretch to fit, or use the original image's size.

3. To change vertical alignment of pictures within the frames, select **Top**, **Middle**, or **Bottom**.

4. For horizontal alignment, select **Left**, **Centre**, or **Right**.

While you can take advantage of PagePlus's preset frames you can create your own shape (e.g., a morphed QuickShape or closed curve) then convert it to a picture frame.

Creating custom picture frames

1. Create the shape as required.

2. Right-click the shape and select **Convert to Picture Frame**.
   OR
   Select **Convert to Picture Frame** from the Tools menu.

You can then add a picture to the frame as described previously.

Using the Media Bar

The **Media Bar** acts as a "basket" containing photos for inclusion in your publication. Its chief use is to aid the design process by improving efficiency (avoiding having to import photos one by one) and convenience (making photos always-at-hand). For photo-rich documents in particular, perhaps based on Photo Album design templates, the Media Bar is a valuable tool for dragging photos directly into picture frames.

You can even go a step further by using the **AutoFlow** feature—this adds all photos sequentially into available empty picture frames with one click.

The bar can be used as a temporary storage area before placing photos in your document, or it can be used to create more permanent photo albums from which you can retrieve stored photos at any time. By default, photos are added to a **temporary album** but remember to click the **New Album** button if you want to save your album for later use. Each time you start PagePlus you simply load that saved album (or any other saved album) or just work with a temporary album—the choice is yours!

Photo albums can be subsequently modified, renamed and deleted—viewing the contents of an individual album or all albums at the same time is possible.

You can import an unlimited number of photos by file or by whole folders, and set photo resolution (native or 96dpi) and whether photos are **embedded or linked** to your project in advance of photo placement on the page.

For large photo collections, searching throughout albums for photos by file name and EXIF, IPTC or XMP metadata is possible; even edit XMP metadata from within PagePlus. See PagePlus help for more information.

 The currently loaded album shown on your Media Bar will remain visible irrespective of which document you have open.

Photo thumbnails can be dragged from the Media Bar directly onto your page, over an existing photo, or into an empty or populated **picture frame**.

To view the Media Bar:
- Unless already displayed, click the ▬▬ handle at the bottom of your workspace.

To add photos to a temporary album:
1. With the Media Bar visible and a temporary album loaded, click on the Media Bar's workspace to reveal an **Open** dialog.

2. From the dialog, navigate to a photo or folder, select photo(s), and optionally choose whether your photos are to be placed at native or 96 dpi, or embedded or linked (embedding may increase your file size significantly).

3. Click **Open**. Your photos appear as thumbnails in the Menu Bar workspace.

 The temporary album and its photo contents will not be saved when you close PagePlus, unless you save it.

To save a temporary album to a named album:

1. Click the down arrow on the button. From the menu, select **New Album**.

2. In the **New Album** dialog, in the **Album Name** box, type a name to identify your album in the future.

3. (Optional) For any photo you can alter the resolution (native or 96 dpi), or embed/link status in advance of placement on your page—click a photo's setting and use the setting's drop-down menu to change. You can also change these settings during drag/drop onto the page.

4. Click **OK**.

The Media Bar is populated with your selected photos.

If you want to include a temporary album's photos in an existing saved album, click the **Add To** button and choose a named album from the menu.

> You can drag one or more files from any Windows folder directly into the Media Bar window.

To create a named album:

1. Click the bar's New Album button.

2. In the dialog, in the **Album Name** box, type a name to identify your album in the future.

3. Use the Add Image... or Add Folder... button to build up the album's photo collection.

4. In the dialog, navigate to a photo or folder and optionally choose whether your photos are to be placed at native or 96 dpi, or embedded or linked (embedding increases your file size significantly). Click **Open**.

5. The **New Album** dialog lists the files for inclusion. Optionally, alter DPI and Embed options by clicking on each photo's setting, then selecting from the drop-down menu.

6. Click **OK**.

To load a saved album:

- Select a saved album name from the bar's top-right drop-down menu. The album's photos will display in the workspace.

To modify a previously saved album:

1. Click the 🪄 Manage button (only shown for existing saved albums).

2. In the dialog, you can add photos/folders, delete photos, change DPI and embed/link status as before. Click **OK**.
   OR
   To add one or more photos, click the 🖼 **Add Image...** button shown on the bar.
   OR
   To add an entire folder of photos, click the 📁 **Add Folder...** button shown on the bar.
   OR
   Right-click in the Media Bar's window and select **Add Images**.

The files are included in the album without having to save manually.

- To delete a photo, select a photo then click the 🖼 **Remove Image** button.
  OR
  Right-click and select **Remove Image**.

- For removal of all photos, select **Remove All Images**.

To rename or delete an album:

- Right-click an existing album name in the top-right drop-down menu and choose **Rename Album...** or **Delete Album...**.

To sort results from an album:

- In the **Sort By** search box, enter your search criteria. Any matching files will be displayed in the bar's workspace.

Adding photos to the page

To add a photo to your page:

1. Display the Media Bar's temporary album or load a saved album from the top-right drop-down menu.

2. Drag an album's photo thumbnail onto the page—either as a detached photo, or directly into a picture frame.
    OR
    Use the **AutoFlow** feature.

> TIP: You can change from embed to link while dragging your photo to the page by using the **Ctrl** or **Shift** key as you drag onto the page (depending on the photo's link/embed status in the album). If you use the **Alt** key at the same time you can also choose to toggle between adding your photo at native or 96 dpi resolution. Your placement cursor will show you how your photo will be added, i.e. embed ⊡, link ⊡, or 96 dpi ⊞.

AutoFlow—adding content automatically

AutoFlow lets you flow the photos currently displayed in the Media Bar throughout empty picture **frames** spread throughout your publication (you can't reflow photos once frames are populated with content). This is especially useful when using Photo Album design templates or other photo-rich documents.

For the feature to work you must have multiple picture frames present in your current document, as well as a range of photos present in your Media Bar. The auto flow process involves a simple click of the mouse button.

To automatically flow your photos:

*   Click the [Auto Flow] button to the right of the bar's workspace. The photos are placed sequentially in your document's available picture frames in the order they appear in the Media Bar.

A dialog will display if you've more picture frames than you have photos and vice versa. To resolve, either remove extra pages or add more frames then add any remaining photos by drag and drop. As a visual aid, a placed photo's thumbnail shows a green tick in its bottom-right corner, while a photo that is not yet placed will not show the tick.

Using the Gallery

The **Gallery** tab serves as a container for storing your own design objects (such as pictures, text blocks, even unlinked text frames or HTML fragments) you'd like to reuse in different publications. It also includes sample designs and (when you install the *PagePlus X2 Resource CD*) is stocked with a wide variety of pre-designed elements that you can customize and use as a starting point for your own designs. Once you've copied a design to the Gallery, it becomes available in any publication—simply open the Gallery!

To view the Gallery tab:

● The **Gallery** tab is by default docked with other tabs. If not displayed, go to **View>Studio Tabs** and select the **Gallery** tab.

The Gallery has two parts: (1) an upper **Categories** group and (2) a lower **Designs** group where you drag designs for storage. The Designs group shows a list of thumbnails representing the designs in the selected category.

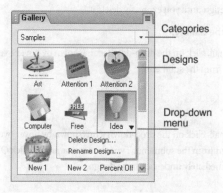

You can maintain your own collection of Gallery designs by adding and deleting items, with the option of naming individual elements to facilitate rapid access.

Each design in the design group can be deleted or renamed from a drop-down menu, available by clicking in the bottom right-hand corner of any design.

To add, delete, or rename Gallery categories:

1. With the Gallery tab selected, click the ▶ **Tab Menu** button and choose **Add category**, **Remove category**, or **Rename category** from the drop-down list.

2. Use the dialog to enter and/or confirm your change.

To move or copy an object into the Gallery:

1. To move, drag the object from the page and drop it onto the Designs group in the right category. To copy, press the **Ctrl** key before starting to drag.

2. If the **Prompt to Rename** option is turned on, you'll be prompted to type a name for the design. (You can name or rename the design later, if you wish.) By default, unnamed designs are labelled as "Unnamed."

3. A thumbnail of the design appears in the Designs group, and its name or label appears below the design.

To use a design from the Gallery:

● Click its thumbnail in the Designs group and drag it out onto the page. The Gallery retains a copy of the design until you expressly delete it.

To delete a design from the Gallery:

● Select a design thumbnail, click on the drop-down icon (shown by hover over) and choose **Delete Design** from the submenu.

Naming designs

To rename a design:

● Select a design thumbnail, click on the drop-down icon (shown by hover over) and choose **Rename Design** from the submenu. Type the new name and click **OK**. The new name appears immediately underneath the design.

Finding designs

To locate a design:

1. Click on the ▶ **Tab Menu** button on the Gallery tab and choose **Find Design....** from the drop-down menu.

2. Type the text to find and click **Find Next**. Starting from the first item displayed, PagePlus searches for the next design (if any) whose name or text includes the search text. The search spans all your Gallery categories.

3. Click **Find Next** to continue the search, or **Close** to exit.

Drawing and editing lines

PagePlus provides **Pencil**, **Straight Line**, **Pen**, and QuickShape tools for creating simple graphics.

Using the **line tools** (found on the Tools toolbar, on the Line Tools flyout), you can draw single lines, connect line segments together, or join line ends to **close** the line, creating a **shape** (see **Drawing and editing shapes** on p. 153 for details). Use the Pointer Tool and the **Curve context toolbar** to resize or reshape lines once you've drawn them.

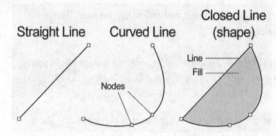

The **Pencil Tool** lets you sketch curved lines and shapes in a freeform way.

The **Straight Line Tool** is for drawing straight lines (for example, drawn in the column gutter to separate columns); rules at the top and/or bottom of the page; or horizontal lines to separate sections or highlight headlines.

The **Pen Tool** lets you join a series of line segments (which may be curved or straight) using "connect the dots" mouse clicks.

Drawing lines

To draw a freeform line (with the Pencil Tool):

1. Click the Line Tools flyout on the Tools toolbar and choose the ✐ **Pencil Tool**.

2. Click where you want the line to start, and hold the mouse button down as you draw. The line appears immediately and follows your mouse movements.

3. To end the line, release the mouse button. The line will automatically smooth out using a minimal number of nodes.

4. To extend the line, position the cursor over one of its red end nodes. The cursor changes to include a plus symbol. Click on the node and drag to add a new line segment.

To draw a straight line (with the Straight Line Tool):

1. Click the Line Tools flyout on the Tools toolbar and choose the ⬈ **Straight Line Tool**.

2. Click where you want the line to start, and drag to the end point. The line appears immediately.

To constrain the angle of the straight line to 15-degree increments, hold down the **Shift** key as you drag. (This is an easy way to make exactly vertical or horizontal lines.)

3. To extend the line, position the cursor over one of its red end nodes. The cursor changes to include a plus symbol. Click on the node and drag to add a new line segment.

To draw one or more line segments (with the Pen Tool):

1. Click the Line Tools flyout on the Tools toolbar and choose the 🖋 **Pen Tool**. On the Curve Creation context toolbar, three buttons let you select which kind of segment to draw:

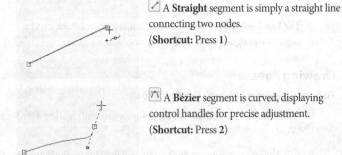

✐ A **Straight** segment is simply a straight line connecting two nodes.
(**Shortcut:** Press **1**)

⌒ A **Bézier** segment is curved, displaying control handles for precise adjustment.
(**Shortcut:** Press **2**)

 **Smart** segments appear without visible control handles, using automatic curve-fitting to connect each node. They are especially useful when tracing around curved objects and pictures.
(**Shortcut:** Press **3**)

2.   Select a segment type, then click where you want the line to start:

- For a **Straight** segment, click again (or drag) for a new node where you want the segment to end. **Shift**-click to align the segment at 15-degree intervals (useful for quick right-angle junctions).

- For a **Bézier** segment, click again for a new node and drag out a **control handle** from it (**1**). (Control handles act like "magnets," pulling the curve into shape. The distance between handles determines the depth of the resulting curved line.) Click again where you want the segment to end, and a curved segment appears (**2**). Pressing the **Shift** key while you're drawing causes the new node's control handles to "snap" into orientation at 15-degree intervals with respect to the node. The finished segment becomes selectable (**3**).

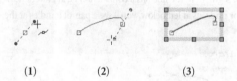

(**1**)   (**2**)   (**3**)

- For a **Smart** segment, click again for a new node. The segment appears as a smooth, best-fitting curve (without visible control handles) between the new node and the preceding node. Before releasing the mouse button, you can drag to "flex" the line as if bending a piece of wire. If the preceding corner node on the line is also smart, flexibility extends back to the preceding segment. You can **Shift**-click to create a new node that lines up at 15-degree intervals with the previous node.

1.   To extend an existing line, repeat Step 2 for each new segment. Each segment can be of a different type.

To select the opposite end node of the curve (i.e., to extend the curve from the other end), press **Tab** before drawing the next segment.

2. To end the line, press **Esc**, double-click, or choose a different tool.

You can reshape the line after it's drawn (see below) or apply different weight, colour, or other attributes (see **Setting line properties** on p. 151).

Editing lines

Use the Pointer Tool in conjunction with the Curve context toolbar to adjust lines once you've drawn them. The techniques are the same whether you're editing a separate line object or the outline of a closed shape.

To move or resize a line:

- Select the line with the Pointer Tool and drag its bounding box to move or resize. When resizing, use the **Shift** key if you wish to keep the line constrained.

To reshape a line:

1. Select a line segment with the Pointer Tool. You'll see the ▶∿ cursor.

2. Drag the line to reshape it. PagePlus automatically applies curve-smoothing to help you achieve a pleasing result.

Selected node(s) will turn orange, and **control handles** for the adjacent line segment(s) will appear. Note that each segment in the line has a control handle at either end, so when you select an **interior node**, as at left below, you'll see a pair of handles at the selected node.

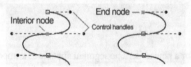

3. Drag the node(s). (**Shift**-drag to constrain the movement to 15-degree intervals.)
   OR
   Adjust one or both of a node's control handles to change the profile of the adjacent segment(s).

Setting line properties

All lines, including those that enclose shapes, have numerous properties, including colour, weight (width or thickness), scaling, cap (end) and join (corner). You can vary these properties for any freehand, straight, or curved line, as well as for the outline of a shape. Note that text frames, tables, and artistic text objects have line properties, too.

To change line properties of a selected object:

- 🖳 Use the Swatches tab to change the line's colour and/or shade. (If changing the outline colour of a shape or other object, click the **Line** button so that the line, not the fill, will change.) Click a gallery sample in the tab's Publication palette or one of the categorized palettes to apply that colour to the selected object. Alternatively, use the Colour tab to apply a colour to the selected object from a colour mixer.

- Use the Line tab or Line context toolbar (shown when a line is selected) to change the line's weight (thickness), type, or other properties. Select a line width, and use the drop-down boxes to pick the type of line. The context toolbar can also adjust line-end scaling as a percentage.

  On the **Line** tab or context toolbar, the middle **Line Styles** drop-down menu provides the following styles: **None**, **Single**, **Calligraphic**, and several **Dashed** and **Double** line styles as illustrated below.

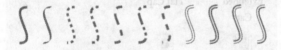

Several techniques offer additional ways to customize lines:

For dashed lines, select from one of five **Dashed** line styles (see above).

-OR-

(Tab only) Drag the **Dash Pattern** slider to set the overall pattern length (the number of boxes to the left of the slider) and the dash length (the number of those boxes that are black). The illustrations below show lines with pattern and dash lengths of (1) 4 and 2, and (2) 5 and 4:

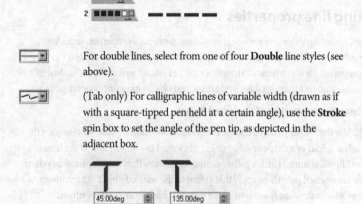

For double lines, select from one of four **Double** line styles (see above).

(Tab only) For calligraphic lines of variable width (drawn as if with a square-tipped pen held at a certain angle), use the **Stroke** spin box to set the angle of the pen tip, as depicted in the adjacent box.

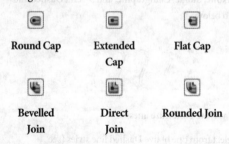

The **Line** tab also lets you vary a line's **Cap** (end) and the **Join** (corner) where two lines intersect. Both properties are more conspicuous on thicker lines; joins are more apparent with more acute angles. The respective button icons clearly communicate each setting:

Round Cap   **Extended Cap**   **Flat Cap**

Bevelled Join   **Direct Join**   **Rounded Join**

To access all Line properties:

- Click the ✎ **Line/Border** button on the Tools toolbar's Fill flyout.

  In the **Line and Border** dialog, the **Line** tab lets you adjust all line properties as described above plus **line end scaling**. **Note:** The **Border** tab (see **Adding borders**) provides a variety of other options for decorative outlines.

- To apply a border to specific edges of the object, use the dialog's **Border Edges** tab.

Controlling line end scaling

For thicker lines that possess line arrow ends, it's sometimes useful to be able to reduce the scaling of the arrow in relation to the line itself. For thin lines, the ability to increase line end scaling—especially if the arrow is not very visible—is essential. Line ends can also be set to be 'internal,' in that they do not extend the line's length but instead occupy a portion of the existing line.

Line end scaling can be applied to freehand, straight and curved lines equally, including connectors (see p. 167).

To adjust scaling:

1. Select a line and click the ⬉ **Line/Border** button on the Tools toolbar's Fill flyout.

2. Increase or decrease the **End scale** percentage value to scale up or down the line end.

3. For a line end that does not extend beyond the line length, check the **Internal line ends** option.

Drawing and editing shapes

PagePlus provides Pencil, Straight Line, Pen, and QuickShape tools for creating simple graphics. **QuickShapes** are pre-designed objects that you can instantly add to your page, then adjust and vary using control handles. Another way to create a shape is to **draw a line** (or series of line segments) and then connect its start and end nodes, creating a **closed shape**. Once you've drawn a shape, you can adjust its properties—for example, apply **gradient or Bitmap fills** (including your own bitmap pictures!) or apply **transparency effects**.

New shapes take the default line and fill (initially a black line with no fill).

QuickShapes

The QuickShape flyout contains a wide variety of commonly used shapes, including boxes, ovals, arrows, polygons, and stars.

To create a QuickShape:

1. Click the **QuickShape** button on the Tools toolbar and select a shape from the flyout. The button takes on the icon of the shape selected.

2. Click on the page to create a new shape at a default size. Drag to adjust its dimensions.

3. When the shape is the right size, release the mouse button. Now you can alter the shape by dragging on its handles.

To draw a constrained shape (such as a circle):

- Hold down the **Shift** key as you drag.

All QuickShapes can be **positioned**, **resized**, **rotated**, and **filled**. What's more, you can adjust them using the **Pointer Tool**. Each shape changes in a logical way to allow its exact appearance to be altered.

To adjust the appearance of a QuickShape:

1. Select it with the **Pointer Tool**. One or more sliding handles appear next to the shape. Different QuickShapes have different handles.

2. To find out what each handle does for a particular shape, move the **Node** tool over the handle and read the Hintline.

3. To change the appearance of a QuickShape, drag its handles.

Closed shapes

As soon as you draw or select a line, you'll see the line's nodes appear. Nodes show the end points of each segment in the line. Freehand curves typically have many nodes; straight or curved line segments have only two. You can make a shape by extending a line back to its starting point.

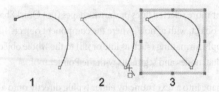

To turn a selected line into a shape:

- Select the line with the **Pointer Tool** and then click the ⊢⋅⊣ **Close Curve** button on the Curve context toolbar.

You can go the other way, too—break open a shape in order to add one or more line segments.

To break open a line or shape:

1. With the **Pointer** tool, select the node where you want to break the shape.

2. Click the ⊢⋅⊣ **Break Curve** button on the Curve context toolbar. A line will separate into two lines. A shape will become a line, with the selected node split into two nodes, one at each end of the new line.

3. You can now use the **Pointer** tool to reshape the line as needed.

Editing shapes

- To move or resize a shape, select it with the **Pointer** tool and drag its bounding box. When resizing, use the **Shift** key if you want to constrain the shape.

- Use **Flip Horizontal** and **Flip Vertical** on the Arrange menu (or right-click menu) to reorient directional shapes like arrows or callouts.

- You can deform an object and (optionally) its fill using the **Mesh Warp flyout** on the Tools toolbar.

- You can adjust an object's crop outline using either the **Square** or **Irregular Crop** tool on the Tools toolbar, or crop a bottom shape to a top shape using **Tools>Crop to Shape**.

- You can convert any shape (such as **artistic text** or a **QuickShape**) to editable lines and nodes using **Convert to Curves** on the Tools menu.

- **Combining** joins two or more selected lines or drawn shapes (not QuickShapes) into a single group-like object, with a "hole" where the component objects' fills overlapped. You can apply formatting (such as line or fill) to the whole object and continue to edit individual nodes and segments with the Pointer tool.

- You can convert any shape into a **text frame** by either typing directly onto a drawn shape (this centres your text vertically and horizontally) or by using **Convert to Shaped Frame** on the Tools menu (text is not auto-aligned). The former method is great for creating objects for diagrams.

- Use the **Weight** slider in the **Line tab** to change the weight (thickness) or type of the shape's border. Click one of the drop-down **Line** options to apply it.

- Use the **Swatches** tab to change the shape's line or fill colour (solid, gradient or bitmap).

- Use the **Transparency** tab to apply a gradient or Bitmap transparency effect.

To access all Line, Fill, and Transparency properties:

- Right-click on the shape and choose **Format>Line and Border...**, **Fill...**, or **Transparency...**. The dialogs let you adjust all Line or Fill properties.

- You can also click the **Fill** or **Line/Border** button on the Tools toolbar's Fill flyout, or the **Transparency** button on the Transparency flyout.

Applying shadows, glow, bevel/emboss, colour fill

PagePlus provides a variety of **"2D" filter effects** that you can use to visually enhance any object. "3D" filter effects, covered later, also let you create the impression of a textured surface. 2D filter effects are especially well adapted to text, as shown here:

Drop Shadow   Inner Shadow   Outer Glow   Inner Glow

Inner Bevel   Outer Bevel   Emboss   Pillow Emboss

To apply a shadow, glow, bevel, or emboss filter effect:

1. Select an object and click the *fx* **Filter Effects** button on the Attributes toolbar.

2. In the **Filter Effects** dialog, apply an effect by selecting its check box in the list at left. For certain effects, also select an effect type from the drop-down list. You can apply multiple effects to a given object.

3. To adjust the properties of a specific effect, select its name and adjust the dialog controls. Adjust the sliders, drop-down menu, or enter specific values to vary the combined effect. (You can also select a slider and use the keyboard arrows. Options differ from one effect to another.

4. Select the **Scale with Object** check box if you want the effect to adjust in proportion to any change in the object's size. With the box unchecked, the effect's extent remains fixed if you resize the object.

5. Click **OK** to apply the effect or **Cancel** to abandon changes.

Colour Fill

The **Colour Fill** effect applies a colour over any existing fill, and lets you achieve some effects that are not possible with other controls. For example, you can use Colour Fill to force everything in a complex group to a single colour, or recolour a bitmap in a solid colour (effectively ignoring everything but the transparency).

Instant shadows

Shadows are great for adding flair and dimension to your work, particularly to pictures and text objects, but also to shapes, text frames and tables. To help you create them in a flash, PagePlus provides the **Shadow Tool** on the Attributes toolbar. The tool affords freeform control of the shadow effect allowing creation of adjustable **basic** or **skewed edge-based shadows** for any PagePlus object.

Basic (left) and skewed shadows (right) applied to a
basic square QuickShape.

Adjustment of shadow colour, transparency, blur, and scaling/distance is possible using controllable nodes directly on the page (or via a supporting Shadow context toolbar). Nodes can be dragged inwards or outwards from the shadow origin to modify the shadow's blur and transparency. For a different colour, select the Colour node then pick a new colour from the Colour or Swatches tab. Depending on if a basic or skewed shadow is required, the origin can exist in the centre (shown) or at the edge of an object, respectively.

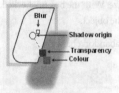

Once you've created a shadow, you can also fine-tune it as needed using the Filter Effects dialog.

To apply a basic or skewed shadow to a selected object:

1. Click the 🔲 **Shadow Tool** on the Attributes toolbar.

2. For a **basic** shadow, with your cursor in the **centre** of the object, drag away to create your shadow.
    OR
    For a **skewed** shadow relative to the Left, Right, Top, or Bottom of the object, select from the **Lock** option on the context toolbar.

3. For either shadow type, continue to adjust shadow position by dragging the shadow's control nodes around until it matches you requirements.

To change a shadow's colour, blur and transparency:

*   For colour adjustment, select the Colour node (e.g., ▨) and either click on a colour on the Colour tab or drag a colour swatch from a Swatches tab's solid colour palette over the node and release.

*   For blur adjustment, drag the small white node further away from the origin for an increasing blur effect and vice versa.

*   For transparency, drag the node between origin and the Colour node further away from the origin for increasing opacity (decreasing transparency) and vice versa.

To change a shadow's position and scaling:

*   For positioning a basic or skewed shadow, increase the context toolbar's **Distance** value to move the shadow away from the parent object and vice versa. For skewed shadows, change the respective **Angle** or **X Shear (Y shear)** value to reposition and shear the shadow by degrees or percentage. **X shear** shows for top/bottom locked shadows, **Y shear** for left/right locked shadows.
    OR
    For basic shadows only, drag the Colour node at the end of the path to the shadow's new position.

*   For scaling a skewed shadow (i.e., stretching the shadow), drag the Colour node at the end of the path to the shadow's new position.

To remove the shadow from an object:

*   Click the **Remove** button from the Shadow context toolbar. You can reapply the object's removed shadow by clicking the tool at a later date.

You can't edit an object's shadow with the Pointer Tool, or detach it from the object. As long as an object has a shadow property, its shadow will simply mirror any changes you make to the object itself.

Using 3D filter effects

3D filter effects create the impression of a textured surface on the object itself. You can use the **Filter Effects** dialog to apply one or more effects to the same object—**3D Bump Map**, **2D Bump Map**, **3D Pattern Map**, **2D Pattern Map** and **3D Lighting** are all available. Keep in mind is that none of these 3D effects will "do" anything to an unfilled object-you'll need to have a fill there to see the difference they make!

Overview

To apply a 3D filter effect to a selected object:

1. Click the _fx_ **Filter Effects** button on the Attributes toolbar.

2. Check the **3D Effects** box at the left. The **3D Lighting** box is checked by default.

See below for details on each effect.

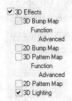

- **3D Effects** is a master switch for this group, and its settings of **Blur** and **Depth** make a great difference; you can click the "+" button to unlink them for independent adjustment.

- **3D Lighting** provides a "light source" without which any depth information in the effect wouldn't be visible. The lighting settings let you illuminate your 3D landscape and vary its reflective properties.

You may wonder why all the 3D effects seem to have "map" in their name. The concept of a **map** is the key to understanding how these effects work: it means a channel of information overlaid on the image, storing values for each underlying fill pixel. You can think of the fill as a picture printed on a flexible sheet, which is flat to start with. Each 3D filter effect employs a map that interacts with the underlying fill to create the visual impression of a textured surface.

Bump Maps superimpose depth information for a bumpy, peak-and-valley effect. Using the flexible sheet metaphor, the bump map adds up-and-down contours and the object's fill "flexes" along with these bumps, like shrink-wrap, while a light from off to one side accentuates the contours.

Pattern Maps contribute colour variations using a choice of blend modes and opacity, for realistic (or otherworldly!) depictions of wood grain, marbling, and blotches or striations of all kinds.

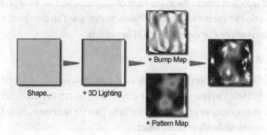

You'll notice that Bump Maps and Pattern Maps come in two varieties: "2D" and "3D." They are all three-dimensional effects-the 2D/3D distinction refers to how each one achieves its result. With the "2D map" variants, you begin by selecting a bitmap from a gallery. With the "3D" Bump Maps and Pattern Maps, you first pick a mathematical function. The function-based maps include data about the interior of the "space," while the bitmap-based maps describe only surface characteristics.

Multiple effects. You can combine multiple 3D filter effects, as in the illustration above. The effects are applied cumulatively, in a standard "pipeline" sequence: 3D Bump > 2D Bump > 3D Pattern > 2D Pattern > 3D Lighting.

The procedures for applying 3D Filter Effects are covered in the PagePlus Help but here's a quick review of each effect type.

3D Bump Map

The **3D Bump Map** effect creates the impression of a textured surface by applying a mathematical function you select to add depth information, for a peak-and-valley effect. You can use 3D Bump Map in conjunction with one or more additional 3D filter effects-but not with a 2D Bump Map.

2D Bump Map

The **2D Bump Map** effect creates the impression of a textured surface by applying a greyscale bitmap you select to add depth information, for a peak-and-valley effect. You can use 2D Bump Map in conjunction with one or more additional 3D filter effects-but not with a 3D Bump Map.

3D Pattern Map

The **3D Pattern Map** effect creates the impression of a textured surface by applying a mathematical function you select to introduce colour variations. You can use 3D Pattern Map in conjunction with one or more other 3D filter effects.

2D Pattern Map

The **2D Pattern Map** effect creates the impression of a textured surface by applying a greyscale bitmap you select to introduce colour variations. You can use 2D Pattern Map in conjunction with one or more other 3D filter effects. (See the **overview** above for background and technical details on these effects.)

3D Lighting

The **3D Lighting** effect works in conjunction with other 3D effects to let you vary the surface illumination and reflective properties.

Feathering

Feathering is a filter effect that adds a soft or blurry edge to any object. It's great for blending single objects into a composition, vignetted borders on photos, and much more. You can apply feathering in conjunction with other filter effects.

To apply feathering:

1. Select an object and choose **Filter Effects...** from the Format menu, or right-click the object and choose **Filter Effects....** The Filter Effects dialog appears.

2. Check the **Feathering** box in the menu shown at the left.

3. Adjust the sliders or enter specific values to vary the feathering effect. (You can also select a slider and use the keyboard arrows.)
    - **Opacity** (0 to 100%) controls the opacity of shadow pixels.
    - **Blur** controls the "fuzziness" of the edge.

4. Check the **Scale with Object** box if you want the effect to adjust in proportion to any change in the object's size. With the box unchecked, the effect's extent remains fixed if you resize the object.

5. Click **OK** to apply the effect to the selected object, or **Cancel** to abandon changes.

Adding dimensionality (Instant 3D)

Using the **Instant 3D** feature, you can easily transform flat shapes (shown) and text into three-dimensional objects.

PagePlus provides control over 3D effect settings such as:

- **bevelling**: use several rounded and chiseled presets or create your own with a custom bevel profile editor.

- **lighting**: up to eight editable and separately coloured lights can be positioned to produce dramatic lighting effects.

- **lathe effects**: create contoured objects (e.g., a bottle cork) with the custom lathe profile editor and extrusion control.

- **texture**: control how texture is extruded on objects with non-solid fills.

- **viewing**: rotate your object in three dimensions.

- **material**: controls the extent to which lighting has an effect on the object's surfaces (great for 3D artistic text!).

An always-at-hand 3D context toolbar hosted above your workspace lets you configure the above settings—each setting contributes to the 3D effect applied to the selected object. For on-the-page object control you can transform in 3D with use of a red orbit circle, which acts as an axis from which you can rotate around the X-, Y-, and Z-axes in relation to your page. Look for the cursor changing as you hover over the red circles' nodes or wire frame.

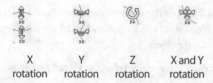

X	Y	Z	X and Y
rotation	rotation	rotation	rotation

TIP: Transform about your 3D objects' axes instead of your pages' axes by holding the **Ctrl**-key down as you transform.

You can also adjust the angle and elevation of each "active" light on the page by dragging the light pointer to a position which simulates a light source.

After any transformation, the underlying base object remains editable.

To add dimensionality:

1. Select an object and click the 🖤 **Instant 3D** button on the Attributes toolbar (or choose **Instant 3D...** from the Format menu). The object immediately adopts 3D characteristics with a red orbit circle displayed in the object's foreground.

2. Click a 3D effect category from the first drop-down menu on the 3D context toolbar; the bar's options change dynamically according to the category currently selected. See the PagePlus Help for more details.

If you're not happy with how your 3D object is looking, you can revert to the object's initial transformation by either clicking the **Reset Defaults** button on the context toolbar or the **Instant 3D** button on the Attributes toolbar.

To switch off 3D effects:

- Click the **Remove 3D** button on the context toolbar. You can always click the Attribute toolbar's **Instant 3D** button at any time later to reinstate the effect.

To edit base properties of a 3D object:

- Select the 3D object, then click the **Edit** button at the bottom right-hand corner of the 3D object, i.e.

The object is shown without its 3D effect, allowing its selection handles to be manipulated for resizing and rotating.

Using object styles

Object styles benefit your design efforts in much the same way as **text styles** and **colour schemes**. Once you've come up with a set of attributes that you like—properties like line colour, fill, border, and so on—you can save this cluster of attributes as a named style. PagePlus remembers which objects are using that style, and the style appears in the Styles tab.

Here's how object styles work to your advantage:

- Any time you want to alter some aspect of the style (for example, change the line colour), you simply change the style definition. Instantly, all objects in your publication sharing that style update accordingly.

- Object styles you've saved globally appear not only in the original publication but in any new publication, so you can reuse exactly the same attractive combination of attributes for any subsequent design effort.

As a bonus, the Styles tab ships with multiple galleries of pre-designed styles that you can apply to any object, or customize to suit your own taste!

Each object style can include settings for a host of object attributes, such as **line colour**, **line style**, **fill**, **transparency**, **filter effects**, **font**, and **border**. The freedom to include or exclude certain attributes, and the nearly unlimited range of choices for each attribute, makes this a powerful tool in the designer's arsenal.

To apply an object style to one or more objects:

1. Display the **Styles** tab.

2. Expand the drop-down menu to display a tree-structure menu showing 3D, Filter effect and Materials categories. Navigate the menu to select a category while previewing available styles as thumbnails in the lower panel.

3. Click a style thumbnail in the panel to apply it to the selected object(s). Drag and drop the thumbnail onto any object.

To create a new object style based on an existing object's attributes:

1. Right-click the object and choose **Format>Object Style>Create**.

   The Style Attributes Editor dialog appears, with a tree listing object attributes on the left and a preview region on the right.

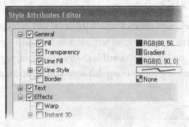

2. Click to expand or collapse sections within the attributes tree. Check any attributes you want to include in the style definition, and uncheck any you don't want to include.

3. If you want to change any of the current object settings, double-click an attribute (or select it and click the **Edit** button). This will bring up a detailed dialog for the particular attribute.

4. The **Object** pane in the preview region shows the currently selected object after applying the defined style. Select the **Artistic Text** or **Frame Text** tab to see the style applied to sample objects of those types.

5. Click the **Browse...** button to select the gallery category where you want to locate the style thumbnail.

6. Type a name to identify the gallery thumbnail.

7. Click **OK**. A thumbnail for the new object style appears in the designated gallery.

Once an object style is listed in a gallery, you can modify it or create a copy (for example, to define a derivative style)by clicking the bottom right-hand corner of its gallery thumbnail and choosing **Edit...**

To remove an object style from a gallery:

- Click the bottom corner thumbnail and choose **Delete** from the drop-down menu.

To unlink an object from its style definition:

- Right-click the object and choose **Format>Object Style>Unlink**.

If you've applied a style to an object but have lost track of the thumbnail—or want to confirm which style is actually being used on an object—you can quickly locate the thumbnail from the object.

To locate an object's style in the Styles tab:

- Right-click the object and choose **Format>Object Style>Locate in Studio**.

The Styles tab displays the gallery thumbnail for the object's style.

Normally, a publication's object styles are just stored locally—that is, as part of that publication; they don't automatically carry over to new publications. If you've created a new style you'll want to use in another publication, you can save it globally so that it will appear in the Styles tab each time you open a new publication.

To save a publication's object styles globally:

- Choose **Save Object Styles** from the Tools menu.

Using connectors

Two **Connector tools** let you create dynamic link lines between any two objects. These connectors remain anchored to the objects, even if either or both of them are moved or resized. So, for example, it's easy to create a flow chart with connectors between boxes, then freely rearrange the layout while preserving the directional relationships!

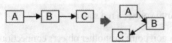

Connector types

The **Connector Tool** lets you draw a single, straight-line connector between any two connection points.

The **Elbow Connector Tool** lets you draw a connector with only vertical and horizontal segments—for example, if you're creating a flow chart, organization chart, or tree diagram.

Connection points

To make connections easy, each PagePlus object has default connection points, displayed whenever you select a Connector tool and hover over a target object. These default points (which can't be moved or deleted) are normally evenly distributed around an object's shape.

To create a connector:

1. For a straight-line connector, select the 🔲 **Connector Tool** on the Connector Tools flyout (Tools toolbar).

   OR

   For an elbow connector, select the 🔲 **Elbow Connector Tool** from the same location.

   Either:

   - Hover over an object so that default **connection points** become visible, e.g. for various shapes.

   OR

   - Hover over an object's edge until you see a red square.

2. Drag from the object's connection point to another object's connection point (default or custom). Release the mouse button when the pointer is over the target connection point. A direct connector will appear between the two connection points.

Instead of using an object's default connection points, you can create your own custom connection points by either hovering over any shape's edge and dragging from that originating point or by simply creating a custom connection point with the **Connection Point Tool**. They can also be placed anywhere on the page, and are especially useful when creating a connection onto grouped QuickShapes or more complex grouped objects such as symbols.

To add a custom connection point (with tool):

1. Select an object.
2. Select the ⊠ **Connection Point Tool** on the Connector Tools flyout (Tools toolbar).
3. Click at a chosen location to place the custom connection point (inside or outside the object). The custom connection point appears in blue.

To view the connection points again you have to hover over the object which was selected while the connection point was created. Remember to enable a Connector Tool in advance.

Editing connection points and connectors

- To **move** a custom connection point, select the object to which it is associated and drag the point with the **Connection Point Tool**.
- To **delete** a custom connection point you've added, use the **Connection Point Tool** to click the object to which the connection point was associated, and then press **Delete**. Default nodes are fixed and can't be deleted.
- To **move**, **reshape**, or **detach/reattach** a connector, use the **Pointer Tool** to drag individual nodes. Drag the end node of a connector to detach or reattach it. (See Drawing and editing lines on p. 147).

If you draw a connector with either or both ends unconnected, the free ends stay anchored to the page as drawn. Of course, you can still move, reattach, or edit the connector just as if it were connected to an object.

As any connector is treated as an ordinary line, you can format it to add arrows, feathers, or other decorative line end.

To format the connecting line:

- To change the line properties, select the connector and display the Line tab. Use the controls to set line thickness, line end, and line dash pattern (see **Setting line properties** on p. 151).

- To change the line colour, use the **Colour tab** or **Swatches tab** (see **Applying solid colours** on p. 173).

- PagePlus lets you scale the connector's line ends in relation to the thickness of the line itself. Choose a **Line end scale** percentage value from the Connectors context toolbar (or go to **End scale** from **Format>Line and Border**). By default, line ends are included as part of the line length (**Internal line ends** option).

Using Colour, Fills, and Transparency

Applying solid colours

PagePlus offers a number of ways to apply solid colours to objects of different kinds:

- You can apply solid colours to an object's **line** or **fill**. As you might expect, QuickShapes and closed shapes (see **Drawing and editing shapes** on p. 153) have both line and fill properties, whereas straight and freehand lines have only a line property.

- Characters in text objects can have fill colour or highlight colour. Text frames and table cells can have a background fill independent of the characters they contain.

- You can colourize a paint-type (bitmap) picture—that is, recolour it to use a different colour. If you recolour a full-colour picture, the colours will convert to tints or shades of the specified colour. You can also apply tinting to a full-colour picture to produce a low-intensity picture (useful for backgrounds behind text).

You can use the Colour tab, Swatches tab or a dialog box to apply solid colours to an object.

To apply a solid colour via the Colour tab:

1. Select the object(s) or highlight a range of text.

2. Click the **Colour** tab from which you can apply colour from one of several colour palettes.

3. Click the ▦ **Fill**, ▦ **Line**, or ▦ **Text** button at the top of the tab to determine where colour will be applied. The colour of the underline reflects the colour of your selected object.

4. Select a colour from the colour spectrum or sliders.

To apply a solid colour via the Swatches tab:

1. Select the object(s) or highlight a range of text.

2. Click the **Swatches** tab.

3. Click the **Fill**, **Line**, or **Text** button at the top of the tab to determine where colour will be applied.

4. Select a colour sample from the Publication palette (colours previously applied to your publication) or Standard palette (supplied preset swatches).

Use **Format>Fill...** to apply colour via a dialog.

- To load a specific palette (such as **Standard CMYK** or **Standard RGB**), choose Palettes from the Tools menu and select palette's name submenu. For more details, see **Managing publication colours and palettes**.

- The top left cell in the colour spectrum (Colour tab) or palette samples (Swatches tab) shows ⊞, which represents either None (a transparent interior for objects with line/fill properties) or Original (for pictures only, to reset the object to its original colours).

Working with gradient and bitmap fills

Gradient fills provide a gradation or spectrum of colours spreading between two or more colours. A bitmap fill uses a named bitmap—often a material, pattern, or background image—to fill an object. PagePlus supplies over 200 preset gradient or bitmap fills on the Swatches tab, and you can import your own. You can recolour bitmap fills using the "Colour Fill" **filter effect**.

Linear   Ellipse   Conical   Bitmap

You can apply gradient and bitmap fills from the Swatches tab to **shapes**, **text frames**, **table cells**, and to the actual characters in **artistic text** objects. Using the **Fill Tool** from the Attributes toolbar, you can vary the fill's path on an object for different effects.

Applying different transparency effects (using the **Transparency** tab) won't alter the object's fill settings as such, but may significantly alter a fill's actual appearance.

Applying a gradient or bitmap fill

There are several ways to apply a gradient or bitmap fill: using the **Fill Tool**, the **Swatches** tab, or a dialog. The dialog lets you add or subtract **key colours** from the gradient, apply different key colours to individual nodes, or vary the overall shading of the effect applied to the object.

To apply a gradient fill with the Fill Tool:

1. Select an object.

2. On the Attributes toolbar, on the Fill flyout, click the 🖉 **Fill** button.

3. Click and drag on the object to define the fill path. The object takes a simple linear fill, grading from its current colour to white.

To apply a gradient or bitmap fill using the Swatches tab:

1. Click the Swatches tab and ensure the 🔳 **Fill** button is selected.

   NOTE: The colour of the underline reflects the colour of your selected object.

2. 🔳 ▾ For gradient fills, select a gradient category, e.g. Linear, Elliptical, etc., from the **Gradient** drop-down list.
   OR

   For bitmap fills, select a category from the 🔳 ▾ **Bitmap** drop-down list.

3. Select the object(s), and then click the gallery swatch of the fill you want to apply.
   OR

   Drag from the gallery swatch onto any object and release the mouse button.

4. If needed, adjust the fill's **Tint** at the bottom of the tab. You can use the slider, or set a percentage value in the input box.

To apply or edit a gradient or bitmap fill using a dialog:

1. Right-click the object and choose **Format** then **Fill** (or select it and choose **Fill...** from the Format menu).
   OR

   On the Attributes toolbar, on the Fill flyout, click the 🖉 **Fill** button.

2. Choose the fill type and category. (You can also use the dialog to apply a solid fill, or no fill.)

• For a two-colour gradient, click the **From** and **To** buttons to specify the gradient's start and end colours. A two-colour gradient has two nodes, one at each end of its path.

• For bitmap fills, select **Bitmap** from the **Type** drop-down list, choose a category, and then click a gallery swatch.

- For gradient fills, select **Gradient** from the **Type** drop-down menu. Click the **Edit** button if you want to add or subtract key colours from the gradient (see **Editing the gradient fill spectrum** below), apply different key colours to individual nodes, or vary the overall shading of the effect applied to the object. You can adjust the fill's shade/tint as needed using the list.

3. Click **OK** to apply the effect or fill to the object.

Editing the fill path

When you select a fillable object, the Fill tool becomes available (otherwise it's greyed out). If the object uses a **gradient fill**, you'll see the **fill path** displayed as a line, with nodes marking where the spectrum between each key colour begins and ends. Adjusting the node positions determines the actual spread of colours between nodes. You can also edit a gradient fill by adding, deleting, or changing key colours (see below).

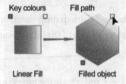

Key colours   Fill path

Linear Fill   Filled object

To adjust the gradient fill path on a selected object:

1. Click the 🖊 **Fill Tool** button on the Attributes toolbar.

2. Use the Fill tool to drag the start and end path nodes, or click on the object for a new start node and drag out a new fill path. The gradient starts where you place the start node, and ends where you place the end node.

Each gradient fill type has a characteristic path. For example, Linear fills have single-line paths, while Radial fills have a two-line path so you can adjust the fill's extent in two directions away from the centre. If the object uses a **bitmap fill**, you'll see the fill path displayed as two lines joined at a centre point. Nodes mark the fill's centre and edges.

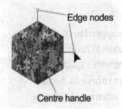

Edge nodes

Centre handle

Unlike the other fill types, bitmap fills don't simply "end" at the edges of their fill path. Rather, they tile (repeat) so you can fill indefinitely large regions at any scale. By dragging the edge nodes in or out with the Fill tool, you can "zoom" in or out on the fill pattern.

For example, these two shapes use identical bitmap fills with different fill path settings:

Nodes far away   Nodes near

To adjust the path of a bitmap fill on a selected object:

1. Click the **Fill Tool** button on the Attributes toolbar. The object's fill path appears.

2. Use the Fill tool to drag the centre and/or edge nodes, or click on the object for a new centre node and drag out a new fill path.

3. To reposition the fill's centre, drag the centre node.

4. To adjust the fill's extent and tiling, drag one or both edge nodes in or out with respect to the centre.

5. To create a skewed or tilted fill region, drag one or both edge nodes sideways.

6. To tilt the fill path in 15-degree increments, hold down the **Shift** key while dragging. The fill path is unskewed and "regularly sized"-that is, its size jumps in steps. To preserve the fill's aspect ratio, hold down the **Ctrl** key. For a combined effect, use both keys together.

   Tip: The **Ctrl**-constrain technique is convenient if you want a bitmap fill to extend to fill a box without tiling. One of the "regular" steps includes a setting where the fill matches the object's bounding box.

Editing the gradient fill spectrum

Whether you're editing a gradient fill that's been already been applied to an object, or redefining one of the gallery fills, the basic concepts are the same. Whereas solid fills use a single colour, all gradient fills utilize at least two **key colours**, with a spread of hues in between each key colour, creating a "spectrum" effect. You can either edit the fill spectrum directly, using the Fill tool in conjunction with the Schemes tab, or use a dialog.

The editing of gradient fills is a complex operation and is covered in full detail in PagePlus Help.

Changing the set of gradient gallery fills

If you've defined a new gradient fill by setting fill path and/or key colours, you can add it to the set of gradient gallery fills shown on the Swatches tab so that it will be available to use again. You can also add new fills or delete any of the existing gallery fills.

To add an object's fill to a fill gallery:

- Right-click the object and choose **Format>Add fill to Studio**.

To define a new gallery fill:

1. Right-click any gallery swatch and choose **Add...**.

2. Use the Object Fill dialog to create your new gradient fill.

3. Click **OK** to accept changes, or **Cancel** to abandon changes.

To delete a gallery fill:

- Right-click its swatch and choose **Delete**.

Deleting a gallery fill doesn't affect any objects that have already been given that fill.

Changing the set of bitmap gallery fills

The Bitmap gallery on the Swatches tab provides a large selection of bitmaps, grouped into categories like Abstract, Material, Patterns, and so on. You can add or delete a bitmap or an entire category.

To add a category to the bitmap fill gallery:

1. Right-click any thumbnail and choose **Add Category**.

2. Type a category name into the dialog, and click **OK**. A new empty gallery category appears.

To delete a category from the bitmap fill gallery:

1.   Choose the category to delete in the drop-down list.

2.   Right-click any thumbnail and choose **Delete Category**.

To add a bitmap fill to the gallery:

1.   Right-click the bitmap thumbnail and choose **Add**.

2.   From the Import Picture dialog, select an image to be your bitmap fill.

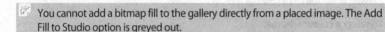

You cannot add a bitmap fill to the gallery directly from a placed image. The Add Fill to Studio option is greyed out.

To delete a bitmap fill from the gallery:

•   Right-click the thumbnail and choose **Delete**.

Deleting a gallery fill doesn't affect any objects that have already been given that fill.

To import a bitmap image file to the bitmap fill gallery:

1.   Choose the category to which you want to add a bitmap.

2.   Right-click any thumbnail and choose **Add**.
     OR
     Click the ⊡ **Tab Menu** button, then choose **Add**. The standard Import Picture dialog appears.

3.   Use the dialog to locate the bitmap image file to import, and click **Open**.

A bitmap thumbnail appears, labelled with the image file name, in the selected gallery.

Setting the default fill

The **default fill** means the fill that will be applied to the next new object you create.

To set local defaults for a particular type of object:

1.   Create a single sample object and fine-tune its properties as desired—or use an existing object that already has the right properties. (For QuickShapes, you can use any QuickShape; all share the same set of defaults.)

2.   Select the object that's the basis for the new defaults and choose **Update Object Default** from the Format menu.
     Right-click the sample object and choose **Format>Update Object Default**.

Using colour schemes

In PagePlus, a **colour scheme** is a cluster of five complementary colours that you can apply to specific elements in one or more publications. The **Schemes** tab displays preset schemes which can be selected at any point during the design process. Each publication can have just one colour scheme at a time; the current scheme is highlighted in the **Schemes** tab. You can easily switch schemes, modify scheme colours, apply schemes to any publication, even create your own custom schemes. Colour schemes are saved globally, so the full set of schemes is always available.

To select a colour scheme:

1. Click the **Schemes** tab. The currently assigned scheme is highlighted in the list.

2. Click a different colour scheme sample. Objects in the publication that have been assigned one of the five colour scheme numbers (see below) are updated with the corresponding colour from the new scheme.

You can repeat this selection process indefinitely. When you save a publication, its current colour scheme is saved along with the document.

How colour schemes work

Colour schemes in PagePlus work much like a paint-by-numbers system, where various regions of a layout are coded with numbers, and a specific colour is assigned (by number) to each region. For example, imagine a line drawing coded with the numbers 1 through 5. To fill it in, you'd use paint from jars also numbered 1 through 5. Swapping different colours into the paint jars, while keeping the numbers on the drawing the same, would produce quite a different painting.

In PagePlus, the "paint jars" are five numbers you can assign to objects in your publication. They're known as "Scheme Colour 1," "Scheme Colour 2," and so on. When you apply Scheme Colour 1 to an object, it's like saying, "Put the colour from jar number 1 here."

- The **Schemes** tab shows the various available schemes, each with a different set of five colours in the five "jars." Whichever named colour scheme you select, that scheme's first colour (as shown in its sample) will appear in regions defined as Scheme Colour 1, its second colour will map to Scheme Colour 2, and so on throughout the publication.

The example below shows three different schemes as applied to a design that's been marked with Scheme Colours 1 through 5 as in the example above.

Applying scheme colours to objects

If you create new elements in a publication to which you have applied a colour scheme, or start a publication from scratch, how can you extend a colour scheme to the new objects? Although you'll need to spend some time working out which colour combinations look best, the mechanics of the process are simple. Recalling the paint-by-numbers example above, all you need to do is assign one of the five scheme colour numbers to an object's line and/or fill.

To assign a scheme colour to an object:

1. Display the **Swatches** tab. The five colours in the current scheme appear as numbered samples at the bottom left-hand corner of the tab. (In Web mode, you'll also see additional samples labelled **H**, **F**, **A**, and **B**, which apply to hyperlink and background colours as detailed in **Choosing Web site colours** on p. 224.)

2. Select the object and click the **Fill**, **Line**, or **Text** button at the top of the tab depending on the desired effect.

3. Click on the scheme colour that you want to apply to the fill, line, or text (or you can drag the colour instead).

If an object's fill uses a scheme colour, the corresponding sample will be highlighted whenever the object is selected.

Modifying and creating colour schemes

If you've tried various colour schemes but haven't found one that's quite right, you can modify any of the colours in an existing scheme to create a new one, or create your own named scheme from scratch.

To modify or create a colour scheme:

1. Select any colour scheme sample in the **Schemes** tab, click on the ▶ **Tab Menu** button and choose **Scheme Manager...** from the drop-down menu.
    OR
    Right-click a sample and choose **Scheme Manager...**.

    The **Scheme Manager** dialog appears, with the current scheme colours shown on the Edit tab.

2. To select a different scheme, switch to the dialog's **Schemes** tab and select a scheme in the scrolling list. Clicking **OK** at this point applies the scheme to the publication, or you can go back to the Edit tab and adjust scheme colours.

On the Edit tab, each of the five scheme colour numbers (plus the Hyperlink, Followed Hyperlink, and background Page Colour if in Web mode) has its own drop-down list, showing available colours in the PagePlus palette.

3. To set or change a scheme colour or adjunct colour, simply click the adjacent button and select a new colour. Click **More Colours...** to display the Colour Selector.

4. To store the modified scheme in the Schemes tab, click **Save Scheme...**. If modifying an existing scheme, leave the name unaltered. If creating a new scheme, enter a new name.

5. To apply the scheme to the current publication (or web site), click **OK**.

Managing publication colours and palettes

Each PagePlus publication has a particular set of colours, known as a **palette**, which appear as a set of gallery swatches in the **Swatches** tab. PagePlus ships with a range of standard palettes, stored separately as files with the .PLT file extension (e.g., **RGB.plt**). New paper and Web publications initially use the standard RGB palette (you can change the default palette if you wish).

Any new colours you create will automatically be added to the Swatches tab (in the **Publication palette**, which hosts other colours previously used in the current publication along with a selection of commonly used colours (e.g., Red, Green, Blue, etc.). Added colours are loaded back into the gallery when you reopen the publication. However, a publication can also include colours that aren't part of its palette, and hence don't appear in the Swatches tab. For example, you might apply a gallery colour to an object and then modify its shade/tint value, creating a unique colour. Any such colours are of course saved in the publication, but they remain separate from the palette itself unless you explicitly add them.

PagePlus lets you quickly load standard RGB, CMYK or "themed" palettes as well as save and load custom palettes for use in other publications.

To add a custom colour to the Publication palette automatically:

● With the Colour tab selected, pick a colour from the displayed colour spectrum.
   OR

● Use the 🖋 **Colour Picker** on the Colour tab to select any colour already on your page. Remember to hold down the mouse button and drag the cursor onto the page.

You can also add colours to the Publication palette by right-clicking on any sample in your Publication palette then selecting the **Add** option, or by using the Palette Manager.

> If you don't want to add colours automatically, uncheck **Automatically Add to Publication** palette on the Colour tab's ▷ **Tab Menu** button.

To add an object's solid fill colour to the Publication palette:

● Right-click the object and choose **Format>Add Fill to Studio**. The colour is added to the Publication palette of the Swatches tab directly.

To edit a specific palette colour in the Publication palette:

1. Right-click a sample in the Publication palette of the Swatches tab and choose **Edit**.

2. Choose a different colour from the colour spectrum in the **Colour Selector** dialog.

3. Click the **OK** button. The colour is updated in the Publication palette.

> Colours present in the standard or "themed" palettes can be edited once added to the Publication palette as above.

> You can also add colours to the Publication palette by right-clicking on any sample in your Publication palette then selecting the Add option, or by using the Palette Manager (see below).

To remove a colour from the publication's palette:

- Right-click on the colour in the Publication palette of the Swatches tab and choose **Delete**. Alternatively, use the Palette Manager.

To load a named palette:

1. In the Swatches tab, click the down arrow on the [■▾] **Palette** button.

2. From the resulting drop-down menu, select a standard (e.g., standard cmyk or rgb) or "themed" palette.

The loaded palette's colours appear as swatches in the Swatches tab, replacing the swatches previously visible.

Using the Colour Selector and Palette Manager

The Palette Manager and Colour Selector are complementary dialogs.

- The **Colour Selector** lets you choose a colour to apply or mix custom colours. Its **Models** tab displays the colour space of several established colour models: RGB (red, green blue), HSL (hue, saturation, luminosity), CMYK (cyan, magenta, yellow, black), and PANTONE® Colours. For all colour models, the values are in the range of 0 to 255. Its **Publication palette** tab lets you modify the set of colours associated with the current publication.

- The **Palette Manager** extends the Colour Selector's Publication palette tab. It not only lets you modify the publication's current palette but also load and save named palettes.

To display the Palette Manager:

- Choose **Palettes** from the Tools menu, then choose **Palette Manager...** from the submenu.

To add a PANTONE® colour to the publication's palette:

- Display the Palette Manager, select **New**, then in the Model list on the **Models** tab choose **PANTONE® Colours**.

PANTONE refers to Pantone, Inc.'s check-standard trademark for colour reproduction and colour reproduction materials. For more details, see PagePlus help.

If you've added new colours to the palette and will want to use them in other publications, you can save the palette.

To save the Publication palette:

- In the Palette Manager, click **Save As...** and specify a name for the palette.

The saved palette's name will appear in the drop-down menu of the **Palette** button (Swatches tab).

Another option if you'll want to use the current palette in another publication is to use the Save Defaults command to record the colour settings globally, so they will be available whenever you create a new publication. For details, see **Updating and saving defaults** on p. 25.

Working with transparency

Transparency effects are great for highlights, shading and shadows, and simulating "rendered" realism. They can make the critical difference between flat-looking illustrations and images with depth and snap. PagePlus fully supports variable transparency and lets you apply gradient or Bitmap transparencies to create your own 32-bit, anti-aliased images. You can export transparent graphics as GIFs, PNGs, or TIFs and preserve transparency effects in both your printed output and your Web pages.

In the illustration below, the pentagonal shape has had a Linear transparency applied, with more transparency at the lower end of the path and less at the upper end. It makes a difference which object is in front (here, the pentagon); where there's more transparency, more of the object(s) behind will show through.

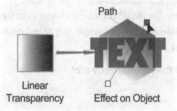

Path

Linear
Transparency

Effect on Object

The concept of transparency

Transparency may seem a bit tricky because by definition, you can't "see" it the way you can see a colour fill applied to an object. In fact, it's there all the time in PagePlus. Each new object has a transparency property: the default just happens to be None—that is, no transparency.

Varying the transparency of an object gives the effect of variable erasure, but it leaves the original object intact-you can always remove or alter the transparency later. Transparencies work rather like fills that use "disappearing ink" instead of colour. A gradient transparency varies from more "disappearing" to less, as in the illustration above. Transparency gallery samples show gradations from light to dark, with the lighter portions representing more transparency.

In PagePlus, the available transparency effects are all comparable to greyscale fills of the same name, and most transparency effects have a path you can edit-in this case, with the Transparency tool.

- **Solid** transparency distributes the transparency evenly across the object.

- **Linear**, **Radial**, and **Conical**, transparencies provide a simple gradient effect, with a range from clear to opaque. (To review the concept, see **Working with gradient and Bitmap fills**).

- The **Bitmap** drop-down menu in the Swatches tab hosts texture maps under a series of categories, including a special category of "Photo Edge Effects" for soft-edge masking.

- At left, a Photo Edge Transparency (with skewed path) on a metafile...

Applying transparency

There are three ways to apply transparency: using the Transparency tool, the **Transparency** tab, or a dialog. The dialog lets you add or subtract nodes from the gradient, reposition nodes, and apply different levels of transparency to individual nodes. (see **Editing transparency effects**).

To apply a transparency effect with the Transparency tool:

1. Select an object.

2. Click the ⬚ **Transparency Tool** button on the Attributes toolbar.

3. Click and drag on the object to define the transparency path. The object takes a simple Linear transparency, grading from opaque to clear.

To apply a transparency effect using the Transparency tab:

1. Click the **Transparency** tab and pick a button (Solid, Gradient, or Bitmap) which will display available transparency samples for the gallery type.

2. Select the object(s) and click the gallery sample for the transparency you want to apply.
   OR

   Drag from the gallery sample onto any object (the cursor changes to include a fill sign over suitable objects), and release the mouse button.

To apply or edit a transparency using a dialog:

1. Right-click the object and choose **Format>Transparency...**.
   OR
   Click the 🖫 **Transparency** button on the Attributes toolbar's Transparency flyout.

2. Choose the desired fill type. In addition:

   • For a **Bitmap** fill, select a desired bitmap transparency category and click a thumbnail.

   • For a **Gradient** effect, select a **Linear**, **Ellipse**, or **Conical** fill.

   • For a simple gradient with two nodes'—one at each end of its path—use the **From** controls to set a starting transparency value, and the **To** controls to set an ending value.

   • Click the **Edit** button to add or subtract nodes from the gradient, or apply different values to individual nodes.

3. Click **OK** to apply the transparency effect to the object.

Editing transparency effects

Once you've applied a transparency, you can adjust its **path** on the object with the 🖫 **Transparency Tool** button.

By clicking the 🖫 **Transparency** button, the level of solid transparency can be adjusted with the Level slider on the Transparency dialog. Likewise, for gradient fills (but not Bitmap fills), you can adjust the **level** of transparency along the path by altering the opacity values of any selected node present on the path—this can be done directly or via the **Transparency** dialog. **Simple** gradient transparency effects have only two nodes, one at each end of the path. **Multi-level** gradient transparency effects include extra nodes along the gradient path.

The process of editing gradient transparencies is the same as that for editing gradient fills (see Editing the fill path on p. 176).

Adding a level of transparency means varying the transparency gradient by introducing a new node and assigning it a greyscale value. For gradient transparencies with multiple nodes, each node has its own level, comparable to a key colour in a gradient fill. You can alter the levels of gradient transparency for any nodes (not those of Bitmap transparencies) to vary the transparency effect.

New node

Effect on Object

Changing the set of gallery transparencies

If you've defined a new gradient transparency by setting path and/or level, you can add it to the set of gallery transparencies shown on the Transparency tab so that it will be available to use again. You can also edit or delete any of the gallery transparencies.

To add an object's transparency to the Transparency tab:

- Right-click the object and choose **Format>Add Transparency to Studio**. The transparency setting is stored as a new sample in the Transparency tab. (a solid transparency is saved to the Solid gallery, gradient to Gradient gallery, etc.).
  OR
  Select the object and choose **Add Transparency to Studio** from the Format menu.
  OR
  Right click a sample transparency in the Transparency tab and select **Add**. Create a transparency from the Transparency dialog.

To edit a gallery transparency:

1. Right-click the sample and choose **Edit**.

2. In the Transparency dialog, choose a new level of transparency with the slider or input box.

3. Click **OK**. The new sample is shown at the end of the samples shown in the Transparency tab.

To delete a gallery transparency:

● Right-click the sample and choose **Delete**.

Deleting a gallery transparency doesn't affect any objects that have already been given that effect.

Setting the default transparency

The **default transparency** means the transparency that will be applied to the next new object you create.

For information on setting defaults in PagePlus, see Updating and saving defaults on p . 25.

Setting the default transparency

Printing your Publication

8

Printing basics

PagePlus supports scaling, tiling, colour separations, and many other useful printing options. Here we'll cover what you need to know for basic desktop printer output. If you're working with a service bureau or professional printer and need to provide PostScript output, see **Generating professional output** (p. 197; which also covers PDF output for professional printing).

To set up your printer or begin printing:

- Click the 🖨 **Print** button on the Standard toolbar.
  OR

- Choose **Print...** from the File menu, or after right-clicking on the page or pasteboard.

The Print dialog appears.

To print:

1. On the **General** tab, select a printer from the list. If necessary, click the **Properties** button to set up the printer for the correct page size, etc.

2. If necessary, click the **Layout**, **Separations**, or **Prepress** tab(s) to set special print options.

   - To set options for scaling, thumbnails, multiple pages, tiling, or mail merge, select the **Layout** tab. For details, see **Printing special formats** on p .195.

   - To specify settings for PostScript colour separations, select the **Separations** tab.

   - To set professional print options select the **Prepress** tab. See **Generating professional output** on p . 197.

3. Select the print range to be printed. If you're printing a **book**, you can select **Entire book** to output all chapters, or **Selected chapters** to output just those you selected. Whichever option you've chosen, a drop-down list lets you export all sheets in the range, or just odd or even sheets, with the option of printing in reverse order.

4. Select the number of copies.

5. The Preview window shows how your publication maps to the selected paper size. You can click the dialog's **Preview** button to hide and show the window.

6. Click **OK**.

Previewing the printed page

The **Print Preview** mode changes the screen view to display your layout without frames, guides, rulers, and other screen items. Special options, such as tiled output or crop marks, are not displayed. A **Trimmed Page mode** can be entered which is similar to Print Preview mode but lets you continue designing without layout aids having to be displayed.

To preview the printed page:

●   Click the 🔍 **Print Preview** button on the Standard toolbar.

In Print Preview mode, the lower toolbar provides a variety of familiar view options, plus the **Multipage** button, which lets you preview your publication using a page array.

To arrange multiple pages in the preview window:

1. Click the ⊞ **Multipage** button. An array selector appears.

2. Move the pointer across the menu to choose an array, e.g. 3x2 Pages. To expand the number of choices, move the pointer to the right and downwards.

3. Click once to make your selection.

To return to single page view:

●   Click the ⊞ **Multipage** button and select the "1x1 Page" array.

To cancel Print Preview mode:

●   Click the **Close** button.

Working in Trimmed Page Mode

Trimmed Page Mode lets you toggle between the page you're currently working on (complete with visible guides, pasteboard objects, text marks, etc.) and a preview page which shows how your page will appear in print. PagePlus takes this useful feature a step further by allowing the page content to be edited whilst still in Trimmed Page mode.

To enter Trimmed Page mode:

- Click the ☐ **Trimmed Page Mode** button on the Hintline toolbar.

Printing special formats

Printing booklets

PagePlus automatically performs **imposition** of folded publications when you use **File>Page Setup...** and select or define a **Folded Publications** type. The settings ensure that two or four pages of the publication are printed on each sheet of paper, with pages printed following the booklet sequence. This saves you from having to calculate how to position and collate pairs of pages on a single larger page, and lets you use automatic page numbering for the booklet pages.

To produce double-sided sheets, use your printer's double-sided option or run sheets through twice, printing first the front and then the back of the sheet (reverse top and bottom between runs). The sheets can then be collated and bound at their centre to produce a booklet, with all the pages in the correct sequence. With complex setups, you may wish to use **commercial printing**.

Printing posters and banners

Posters and banners are large-format publications where the page size extends across multiple sheets of paper. To have PagePlus take care of the printing, set up your publication beforehand using File/Page Setup... (with the **Large Publications** option) to preview and select a particular preset arrangement.

Even if the publication isn't set up as a poster or banner, you can use tiling and scaling settings (see "Tiling" below) to print onto multiple sheets from a standard size page. Each section or tile is printed on a single sheet of paper, and the various tiles can then be joined to form the complete page. To simplify arrangement of the tiles and to allow for printer margins, you can specify an overlap value.

Scaling

- Under "Special Printing" on the Print dialog's **Layout** tab, set the "As in document - % Scale factor" option to specify a custom scaling percentage. The default is 100% or normal size. To scale your work to be printed at a larger size, specify a larger value; to scale down, specify a smaller value. Check **Fit Many** to have PagePlus fit as many pages as possible on each sheet—for example, two A5 pages on a landscape A4 sheet.

- Set "Scale to fit paper size" values to adjust artwork automatically to fit neatly on the printed page.

- Note that the Fit Many option ignores printer margins, while Scale to Fit takes them into account. So if you use Fit Many, make sure your page layout borders don't extend beyond the printable region.

Printing thumbnails

- Under "Special Printing" on the Print dialog's **Layout** tab, set the "Print as thumbnails" option to print multiple pages at a reduced size on each printed sheet, taking printer margins into account. Specify the number of thumbnails per sheet in the value box.

PagePlus will print each page of the publication at a reduced size, with the specified number of small pages or "thumbnails" neatly positioned on each printed sheet.

Multiple pages

- Under "Multiple pages per Sheet" on the Print dialog's **Layout** tab, select an option.

The multiple page options are enabled when you are working with a page from the Small Publications category in Page Setup. You can select the number of times to repeat each page, and tell PagePlus to skip a certain number of regions on the first sheet of paper. Skipping regions is useful if, for example, you've already peeled off several labels from a label sheet, and don't want to print on the peeled-off sections. Check the Preview window to see how the output will look.

- If you haven't set up the publication as a Small Publication, but still want to print multiple pages per sheet, try using the **Fit Many** option (see "Scaling" above). Note that this option ignores printer margins and doesn't change the imposition (orientation) of output pages.

Tiling

- Under "Tiling" on the Print dialog's **Layout** tab, check the **Print tiled pages** option to print large (or enlarged) pages using multiple sheets of paper.

- Set the **% Scale factor** to print at a larger size (e.g. 300%)

Each section or tile is printed on a single sheet of paper; the various tiles can then be joined to form the complete page. Use this option for printing at larger sizes than the maximum paper size of your printer, typically for creating banners and posters. To simplify arrangement of the tiles and to allow for printer margins, you can specify an overlap value.

Generating professional output

Beyond printing your own copies on a desktop printer, or having copies photo reproduced at a quick print shop, you may wish to consider professional (typically offset) printing. For example, if you need to reproduce more than about 500 copies of a piece, photocopying begins to lose its economic advantages. Or you may need **spot colour** or **process colour** printing for a particular job. You can output your PagePlus publication and hand it off to any trusted commercial printer.

If you're not using colour matching, we suggest you set up **ICC device profiles**: for image colours and enable **colour management** so that images in the exported file include correct colour space information. You can also specify a device profile for your desktop printer for accurate on-screen proofing of desktop-printed colours. For details, see Managing screen and output colours in PagePlus help.

Unless you're handing off camera-ready artwork, your print provider will specify the format in which you should submit the publication: either **PDF/X** or **PostScript** (see Online Help). Once you've decided whether to output as PDF or PostScript, you'll need to set Prepress options before choosing the appropriate output command.

The Separation and Pre-press options are further described in the PagePlus Help. In addition, the process for producing colour separations is detailed.

PDF/X

PDF is a format developed by Adobe to handle documents in a device- and platform-independent manner. PDF excels as an electronic distribution medium and the reliable **PDF/X** formats are perfect for delivering a publication file to a professional printer. Your print partner can tell you whether to deliver PDF/X-1 or PDF/X-1a (PagePlus supports both)—but from the PagePlus end of things you won't see a difference. In either mode, all your publication's colours will be output in the CMYK colour space, and fonts you've used will be embedded. A single PDF/X file will contain all the necessary information (fonts, images, graphics, and text) your print partner requires to produce either spot or process colour separations.

To output your publication as a PDF/X file:

1. Choose **Publish as PDF...** from the File menu.

2. Review General and Advanced tab settings (see **Exporting PDF files** on p. 201).

When preparing a PDF/X file for professional printing, choose either "PDF X/1" or "PDF X/1a" in the General tab's **Compatibility** list, as advised by your print partner. Also inquire whether or not to **Impose pages**; this option is fine for desktop printing of a folded publication or one that uses facing pages, but a professional printer may prefer you to leave the imposition (page sequencing) to them.

3. Review **Prepress tab** settings.

You don't need to worry about the Compression or Security tabs; these only apply to standalone PDFs.

Saving print profiles

You can save the current combination of settings made in the Print dialog as a **print profile** with a unique name. Note that the profile includes settings from all tabs except the Separations tab. (By the way, don't confuse these PagePlus "print profiles" with ICC "device profiles."

To save current print settings as a print profile:

*   On the Print dialog's **General** tab, click the **Save As...** button next to the Print Profile list.

*   Type in a new name and click **OK**.

The settings are saved as a file with the extension .PPR.

You can restore the profile later on simply by choosing its name in the list.

Publishing and Sharing

9

Publishing and
Sharing

Exporting PDF files

PDF (short for Portable Document Format) is a cross-platform file format developed by Adobe. In a relatively short time, PDF has evolved into a worldwide standard for document distribution which works equally well for electronic or paper publishing—including professional printing. In recent years, print shops are moving away from PostScript and toward the newer, more reliable **PDF/X** formats expressly targeted for graphic arts and high quality reproduction. Several different "flavours" of PDF/X exist; PagePlus supports PDF/X-1 and PDF/X-1a.

To export your publication as a PDF file:

1. Prepare the publication following standard print publishing guidelines, and taking the distribution method into account.

2. (Optional) Insert **hyperlinks** as needed, for example to link table of contents entries to pages in the document..

3. (Optional) To create **pop-up annotations**, insert PageHints as needed.

4. (Optional) Once the publication is final, prepare a bookmark list (see **Creating a PDF bookmark list** on p. 202).
   Note: Bookmarks appear as a separate list in a special pane when the PDF file is viewed. They can link to a specific page or to an **anchor** (for example, a piece of text or a graphic object) in your publication.

5. Choose **Publish as PDF...** from the File menu and check your export settings. (To export the whole publication using default settings, you won't need to change any settings.) For a detailed explanation of each export setting see PagePlus Help.

6. Click **OK** to proceed to export.

If you checked **Preview PDF file in Acrobat**, the resulting PDF file appears in the version of Adobe Acrobat Reader installed on your system.

 TIP: You can insert sound and movie clips in your publication which will play in your exported PDF. Choose options from the **PDF Media Clip>** located on the Insert menu.

Creating a PDF bookmark list

Bookmarks are optional links that appear in a separate pane of the Adobe Reader when a PDF file is displayed. Typically, a bookmark links to a specific location such as a section heading in the publication, but it can also link to a document page. You can insert bookmarks by hand, or PagePlus can apply **automatic generation** to produce a nested bookmark list up to six levels deep, derived from named styles in your publication.

A **Bookmark Manager** enables you to view all your bookmarks at a glance, organize them into a hierarchy of entries and subentries, and modify or delete existing bookmarks as needed.

To use styles to automatically generate bookmarks:

1. Decide which named styles you want to designate as headings at each of up to six levels.

2. Check your publication to make sure these styles are used consistently.

3. Choose **Bookmark Manager...** from the Tools menu and click **Automatic...**.

In the dialog, you'll see a list of all the style names used in your publication.

4. Check boxes to include text of a given style as a heading at a particular level (1 through 6). For example, you could include all text using the "Heading" style as a first-level heading. To remove all bookmarks in the list, clear all check boxes.

5. Click **OK** to generate bookmarks.

The mechanics of **creating a PDF bookmark list by hand** are simple. For example, to create a basic list with bookmarks to section heads, you simply proceed forward through the publication, inserting a bookmark for each heading. Bookmarking a specific location (for example, a piece of text or a graphic object) entails placing an **anchor** at that location; the anchor serves as the target for the bookmark link.

To insert bookmarks by hand:

1. (Optional) To bookmark a specific location in the publication, first place the cursor at that point or select an object. You can select a range of text (for example, a section heading) to use it as the actual text of the bookmark.

2. Press **Ctrl+R** or choose **Bookmark...** from the Insert menu (or Insert Bookmark... from the right-click menu).
    OR
    Choose **Bookmark Manager...** from the Tools menu. In the bookmark tree, display the entry below which you want to create the new bookmark. (Check **Create as sub-entry** if you want the new bookmark nested as a "child" of the selected entry.) Then click the **Create...** button.

3. In the Create Bookmark dialog, the **Text** field shows the range of text you selected if any (for example, a section heading). You can leave this if it's suitable for the bookmark text or edit it as needed; otherwise enter new text if the field is empty.

4. Click to select the bookmark destination type, then enter the destination.
    • To bookmark a specific location, choose **An anchor in your publication**. To place a new anchor at the cursor location, select <**Anchor at current selection**> from the list below. You'll be prompted to enter an anchor name (with the bookmark text as the default); edit the name if you like and click **OK**. To bookmark a previously placed anchor, simply choose it from the list.
    • To bookmark a specific page in the publication, select **A page in your publication** and select the target page number.

5. Click **OK** to confirm your choices.

Unlike **hyperlinks**, bookmarks also work as actual links within PagePlus publications. You can use the Bookmark Manager as a jumping-off point to any bookmarked entry.

Creating a PDF slideshow

The creation of PDF slideshows takes PagePlus's PDF publishing a step further. While a PDF file shows the exact replication of your original project for electronic distribution or printing, the PDF slideshow feature does the same, but with the intention of creating automated multimedia presentations. These can be shared by email and viewed without the need for special presentation software.

The main features of PDF slideshow include:

- Advance of each slide manually or automatically.

- Creation of multi-section slides from individual PagePlus pages.

- Use of slide-specific layer control (switch layers on or off).

- Freedom to reorder your slideshow.

- Apply slide-specific transition effects.

- Control of slide duration.

- Play a soundtrack for single slides or for the entire slideshow.

To publish a slideshow:

1. Select **Publish as PDF Slideshow...** from the File menu.

2. In the dialog, on the **General** tab, choose a default **Transition** type for all slides, e.g. Blinds, Wipe, or Dissolve. An individual slide can override this setting with its own transition setting.

3. Check **Manual Advance** if you don't want your slideshow to display slides one by one automatically—slides will be progressed manually by mouse-click or by pressing the space bar. For automatic slideshows, choose a **Duration**, i.e. the number of seconds each slide will remain on screen.

4. Uncheck **Preview PDF file in Acrobat** if you don't want to see a slideshow preview immediately after publishing.

5. When your slideshow reaches the last page you can **Loop slideshow** for continuous play or **Return to normal view** to exit the slideshow.

6. In the **Compatibility** field, select a version of Acrobat Reader. You'll get best results by using the latest version, but if your intended audience is unlikely to have the latest Reader software, you may opt for an earlier version.

7. For accompanying music, in the **Media** box, click the **Open** button to navigate to and select an audio file (WAV, MP3 and AIFF files supported).

8. For multi-section slides, from the **Slides** tab, duplicate or copy a selected slide with the **Insert** or **Copy** button, respectively. Delete a slide if needed, or rearrange the playback order of existing slides with the **Up** or **Down** buttons. For more information, see **Multi-section slides** (see p. 205).

9. The Compression, Security and Advanced tabs are as described in **Exporting PDF files** (see p. 201), and should be set accordingly. For most slideshows, the Compression tab's **Downsample Image** option should be checked and set to 96dpi (suitable for on-screen display).

10. Click **OK**. In the dialog, save your named PDF file to a chosen location. If **Preview PDF file in Acrobat** was checked, your slideshow will start to run automatically.

Use the **Reset** button to revert your slide settings so slides match your PagePlus pages again.

Multi-section slides

One strength of the slideshow feature comes from the ability to make multi-section slide variants based on a single PagePlus page (this is done by control of the page's layers). This is fantastic when it makes sense to reuse most of the original page's content—simply create slides based on the original page then edit them by switching on/off specific layers to create unique slides. A few examples...

● Create time-delayed bulleted lists—great for mouse- or pointer-driven presentations.

● Introduce artistic elements to your page over time

● Change photos over time

As you have full control over each slide's layers, you can design simple to complex designs based on which layer objects you choose to adopt. This, and the ability to assign different transition types and slide durations per slide, means that you have in-built flexibility when designing your slideshow. Your original PagePlus document needs to be designed with this in mind.

You may like to visit the Design Template category called PDF from which you can base your own slideshow.

To create multi-section slides:

1. In the **Slides** tab of the **Publish PDF Slideshow** dialog, choose a page from which you want to create a slide and click the **Insert** or **Copy** button. The former inserts a chosen slide above the currently selected slide as a copy; the latter simply places a copy above a selected slide.

2. Select the new slide and click the **Properties** button.

3. Set a slide-specific **Transition** and **Duration** (in seconds) from the drop-down menus.

4. Uncheck any layers which you don't want to be part of the slide to make it distinct from other slides.

5. Click the ⬚ browse button and then browse to and select a **Media** file, which will play while the slide is displayed. For the slide's duration, this will override any default media file set up to play throughout your slideshow.

6. Repeat the insert, copy, and layer control for another slide, building up your multi-section slide arrangement.

Sharing by email

The widespread availability of the Internet means that colleagues, family and friends are now only a quick email away. Higher line speeds via Broadband connections open up new opportunities for sharing publications either as native PagePlus publications (.PPP) or as HTML. PagePlus will create an email from your standard email program (e.g., Outlook) either as a file attachment or within the body of your email, respectively.

Sharing PagePlus publications

1. With your publication open and in the currently active window, select
    Send... from the File menu.

    If the email program is not loaded, a Choose Profile dialog lets you select your
    email program, then a new email message is displayed with document
    attached. If already loaded, your email program automatically attaches your
    publication to a new email message.

2. Add the recipient's valid email address to the **To...** field (or equivalent).

3. Select the **Send** button (or equivalent) on your email program as for any other
    email message.

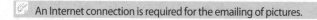 An Internet connection is required for the emailing of pictures.

Interested in sharing content with recipients who may not be using PagePlus? The **Send
page as HTML** feature lets you dispatch any page, safe in the knowledge that the email
recipient(s) will be able to view your content exactly as intended (including all pictures
and hyperlinks) because all referenced images are embedded locally with the message.
This is a great method for publicising your publication (send your title page), providing
work examples, email-ready photo albums or even datasheets.

 If you'd like to create blogs, birthday invites, holiday photo albums, or business
emails you can save time by adopting an email-ready design template (click on
use a design template in the **Startup Wizard**).

Sharing as HTML

1. With your publication open, select the page you would like to send.

2. Select **Send page as HTML...** from the File menu. The page is added to the
    body a newly created HTML-based email message.

3. Add the recipient's valid email address to the **To...** field (or equivalent).

4. Select the **Send** button (or equivalent) on your email program.

This method shares a single page only. To share a multi-page publication with
recipients who don't use PagePlus, consider outputting your project as a PDF
and then send the PDF as an attachment.

To use this feature you (or any recipient intending to reply or forward) must be operating Microsoft Outlook or Outlook Express as your email program, with the **Use Microsoft Word to edit email messages** option in Outlook settings unchecked (see Tools>Options>Mail Format).

Using PDF Forms

Using PDF Forms

Getting started with PDF forms

The continuing development of Adobe's® Acrobat® technology means that great new possibilities are available to PagePlus. One of the most exciting is the use of electronic-based PDF forms—these allow information to be collected from readers of your publication in an efficient and modern manner. In much the same way as traditional paper forms are used to collect information (remember your last Tax Return!), PDF forms offer the same form completion concepts, but increase the interactivity between publisher and audience by using an electronic medium.

Some common form types include Application forms, Contact Information forms, Request forms, Feedback forms and Guest books.

One thing in common with all PDF forms is that they have to be published as PDF to operate. A PagePlus .PPP file with form functionality must be converted to PDF with **File>Publish as PDF**.

Form Structure

The building blocks of a form comprise a mixture of text, graphics and **Form fields**. Form fields collect recipient data and can be added, moved and modified in a similar way to more familiar objects in PagePlus such as graphics and table elements. A field can be a Text field, Radio Button, Combo box, List box, Check box or a simple button.

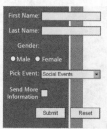

From the form recipient's perspective, information is typed into **text boxes** or selected from **check boxes**, **radio buttons**, or **drop-down boxes**. The information entered can be numeric, textual, or a mixture of both. It is possible to arrange and lock form fields, plus control the order in which form fields can be navigated (see Designing your PDF forms in PagePlus Help).

Each field has its own set of **Form Field Properties** relating to its appearance, its value(s), validation, calculations, and the action expected of the field.

In PagePlus, the form should be integrated into your Page design as you develop your publication. The form's functionality only then becomes active when a PDF of the form is generated. When a form recipient enters data into form fields the data can be collected as described below.

JavaScript is used to allow interactivity in your PDF forms. It drives formatting, validation, calculations, and actions—all key functions in PDF form development.

How is data collected?

Several methods exist for collecting forms once they have been completed.

(1) By Hardcopy **Print.**

(2) You can **Save Data to e-mail** (alternatively you can save data within the form).

(3) You can **Submit Data to Web** (a CGI application; by submission to a web-enabled server/database).

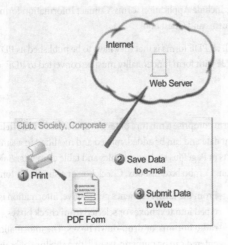

Creating PDF forms

Adding form fields

A series of form fields can be added to the page, depending on the type of form you want to create. Typically a mix of form fields will make up your finished form design.

Fields are created from the Form toolbar or via **Insert>Form Field**. You assign an internal unique name to each field and then set a variety of properties. Each form field has its own set of **Form Field Properties** which can be modified to suit your form implementation.

Icon	Form Field Name	When to use?
	Button*	Use when specifying an action that can be triggered by a button click.
	Submit button*	Use when sending the form recipient's completed form data to **Serif Web Resources** or to your own **Web server**. A Form Submit Wizard is activated to enable quick and easy button setup.
	Reset button*	Use when you want to add a button to clear all form fields of data (often complements the above Submit button).
	Print button*	Use when you want to add a print button to your form.
	Check Box	Ideal when you want to multiply select a series of options displayed side by side. A good alternative to a Combo Box or List box if space allows.
	Text Field	Use for adding text, numbers or a mixture of both.
	Combo Box	For selection from a scrollable list of items in a drop-down menu where only one item can be selected (**example**). The box also allows data entry to be input into this box type. Smaller than a List Box.
	List Box	For selection from a scrollable list of items; supports multiple selection and advanced actions on selection of menu items.
	Radio Button	Good for selection of a single mutually exclusive item from a grouped subset of choices.
	Signature	Used for the digital signing of secure documents. See PagePlus Help.

* This button shares a drop down menu with other buttons marked with an asterisk. The button type previously chosen will always be display on the Form toolbar.

To add a form field:

1. Select one of the form field buttons on the **Form** toolbar.

2. Move your ✛◼ cursor to the location at which you want to place your form field and click once.

3. Right-click on the form field and choose **Form Field Properties** from the drop-down menu.

4. In the **General** tab, overwrite the current **Name** with a unique internal name. You can also choose several other optional settings (see General tab).

5. Go to the **Options** tab, and choose enter a new Caption name.

6. (Optional) Go to the **Actions** tab and click the **Add** button.

7. (Optional) In the resulting Action dialog, select an Event that will be used to trigger the action.

8. (Optional) Choose an **Action** from the drop-down menu.

9. (Optional) Change the properties displayed under the selected action. The options shown change depending to the action selected.

Form field properties

Form field properties control how the form field will operate when the form recipient enters their input. A series of tabs are arranged so that some tabs, e.g. **General**, **Appearance**, **Options**, or **Actions**, are common to all the form fields but others, such as **Format**, **Validation** and **Calculations** are only displayed for text fields and combo boxes.

To access Form Field Properties:

1. To view the properties do one of the following:

    *   Right-click on a selected form field and choose **Form Field Properties**.

    *   Double-click the form field.

    *   Select the form field, and click the 🖻 button from the **Form** toolbar.

2. Click on one of several tabs for editing: General, Appearance, Options, Actions, Validate, or Calculate.

3. Click the **OK** or **Cancel** button to exit the dialog.

Publishing your PDF Form

Once your PDF form is completed you can publish the form using **File>Publish as PDF**. See **Exporting PDF files** on p. 201 for more information.

 If you Publish as PDF using PDF/X-1 or PDF/X-1a compatibility, any PDF form fields present will be converted to graphics and will not be available. Choose an Acrobat option instead.

Collecting data from forms

Via Hardcopy Printout

This is a simple fill-in and print to hardcopy solution. This is great if your form recipients are located together, perhaps in the same office.

 If using Acrobat® Reader®, any completed form data will be lost when you close your completed PDF form. Exceptions exist when using Standard or Professional software.

Within the PDF File

Alternatively, it is possible to store form data within the PDF Form itself by using the **Save** or **Save As...** command. One condition of this is that the form recipient must be using one of the following versions of Acrobat software:

- Adobe® Acrobat® 6.0 (or later) Standard or Professional

- Adobe® Acrobat® 7.0 Elements

 Acrobat® Reader® software (6.0 and above) is unable to save form data within the form. However, for form recipients with Acrobat® Reader® 7.0 software, **Adobe® LiveCycle™ Reader Extensions** software is available from Adobe which will permit form data to be saved locally with the form. This is called rights-based PDF Form handling.

Using email

If you can save data within the PDF form then it's clear that you can email the completed form to the form originator. With the completed form still open, use **File>Email** to send the email to the intended recipient.

Via the Web

Your PDF Form can be configured to be Web ready by passing completed form data to a CGI application on a Web server. This would typically be a server-sided web page designed to process the data and pass it to a text file, database or other storage location. As an example, new subscriber details, collected via a PDF Form, can be sent automatically to a previously configured "subscribers" database.

All Web-ready forms have one thing in common—they must be submitted to allow data to be collected. Typically, you may have come across this on web sites when you enter details into a form then submit the data by pressing a Submit button. The same applies for PDF forms—a **Submit** button can be configured in order to submit the form data to the Web server. You can either create the button unaided or use the **Form Submit Wizard** (see below). Either way, the use of the submit process is the major difference between web-ready and other less dynamic forms.

The Web process, as mentioned, requires a Web server to operate. Not everyone will have access to or even want to operate their own Web server so, as an alternative to this, you can use **Serif Web Resources**. This is a free Web to email gateway service which will collect your valued form data at Serif and send it to your email address—the service does require that you firstly have a Customer login (for security reasons), which will allow you to create, edit and delete Form IDs via a web page accessible from the Wizard. The Form ID, a unique 30-digit number, is required for the service to operate and is generated automatically when you enter your destination email address in the above web page.

 No personal data will be stored on Serif Web servers. All form data is redirected in real time.

Submitting Form Data

The submission of form data sounds a very complicated operation but by using a Form Submit Wizard the process is relatively straightforward. The Wizard not only creates a Submit button for your form, but configures the underlying submit process and the format in which your form data is to be stored in.

The submit process is made either to Serif Web Resources or to your own Web server address (e.g., http://testserver.global.com/forms/collect.asp).

Form data can be stored in several data formats:

Data Format	via Serif Web Resources	To Web Server
HTML	ASCII. The form data can be read directly in your email without acrobat software.	ASCII. Use for sending form data directly to the Server-sided Databases, as in Web forms.
FDF	The form data is emailed as an attachment, and when opened, is reunited with the original form to allow data to be read In Situ.	binary. The form data can be stored on the web server.
XFDF	As for FDF but with additional XML-based support.	binary. The form data can be stored on the web server.
PDF	Not available.	binary. The form data can be stored on the web server. Useful for preserving digital signatures.

To run the Form Submit Wizard:

1. Select the ⬚ **Submit** button from the Button flyout menu on the **Form** toolbar.

2. In the first step, start the wizard by clicking the Next> button.

3. Choose either Serif Web Resources or your own server as the destination of your form recipient's data. The former is appropriate if you don't have access to your own web server. Depending on your choice, you can:

    1. For Serif Web Resources, click Next>.

    2. Click the Get a Form ID button to display Serif's customer login web page. This page is where you log onto your customer account to enter firstly your email address to send form data to, and secondly to generate a unique Form ID for use in the secure email communication.

3.   At the web page, if you already have a customer login you can enter your email address and password. For new customer you must register before continuing.

4.   After login, select the add form link to enter the email address that you want your form data to be sent to.

5.   Click the Add Form button. This generates an entry in the displayed list from which a 30-digit Form ID can be copied.

6.   Paste the Form ID directly from the web page into the input field in your Wizard dialog.

7.   Click the Next> button.

8.   Select a Data format from the drop-down menu that you would like to store and transport your form data. Select one of: HTML, FDF, or XFDF (see p. 217).

OR

1.   **For your own Web server,** click Next>.

2.   Add your Web Server address to the displayed field, click Next>.
     NOTE: This should not be a file directory but a valid Web site on the Intranet/Internet.

3.   Choose a data format for exporting the form data. Select one of: HTML, FDF, PDF or XFDF.
     NOTE: You must ensure that your server is able to process the above data formats.

4.   Finish the Wizard process by clicking the **Finish** button.

5.   Move your ✛■ cursor to the location for your button and click once.

The Submit button settings can be edited (as for other form fields) by right-clicking and selection of Form Field Properties. This will allow form fields to be included/excluded from data collection.

You can import FDF form data previously submitted to another PDF form as explained in PagePlus help.

Producing Web
Pages

Getting started in Web mode

How easy is it to create your own Web site with PagePlus? It can be as simple as selecting a preset design template and editing the headings and accompanying text. And no matter how much customizing you choose to do after that, the whole job won't be nearly as complicated as developing your own site from first principles. So, if you're already comfortable using PagePlus for paper publications, you'll find it easy going. If you're just beginning, you'll learn to use PagePlus tools as you go.

Essentially, PagePlus takes the pages you've laid out and converts them to HTML. In fact, the Web design templates simplify things further by providing you with a variety of starter layouts, professionally designed expressly for World Wide Web display.

It's possible to perform more advanced web design including addition of search engine descriptors, insertion of HTML code, and rollover graphics. These subjects are covered in more detail in PagePlus help.

Starting a new Web publication

Paper Publishing mode is the familiar PagePlus environment for creating print publications. However, before developing your web site PagePlus must operate in **Web Publishing mode**. The Web Publishing mode includes special features, such as menu items and custom settings, to facilitate creation of World Wide Web pages.

 If you choose any of the Web Page design templates after starting PagePlus you will be in Web Publishing mode automatically.

To create a new Web publication using a Page Wizard:

1. Launch PagePlus or choose **New>New from Startup Wizard** from the **File** menu.

2. In the Startup Wizard, select the **Use a design template** option, select the **Web Publishing** category on the left, and examine the samples on the right. Click the sample that's closest to the site you want to create, then click **Open**.

Just as in Paper Publishing mode, you also have the option of starting a new publication from scratch, or opening an existing publication.

If you'd like to build on previous work you've done with PagePlus, you can also take an existing paper publication and convert it to a Web publication.

To turn an existing PagePlus (paper) publication into a World Wide Web site:

- Open the publication in Paper Publishing mode and choose **Switch to Web Publishing** from the File menu.

Hyperlinking an object

Hyperlinking an object such as a box or **Quick Button**, a word, or a picture means that a visitor to your Web site can click on the object to trigger an event. The event might be a jump to a Web page (either on your site or somewhere else on the Web), the appearance of an email composition window, or the display of a graphic, text, audio, or video file. Hyperlinking enables visitors to navigate through your Web site or **PDF document**.

To hyperlink an object:

1. Use the **Pointer Tool** to highlight the region of text.

2. Click the 🖳 **Hyperlink** button on the Standard toolbar, or choose **Hyperlink...** from the Insert menu.

3. In the **Hyperlinks** dialog, click to select the link destination type, and enter the specific hyperlink target—an Internet page, a page on your Web site, an email address, or local file.

4. Click **OK**.

As a visual cue, hyperlinked words are underlined and appear in the colour you've specified in the Scheme Manager.

To modify or remove a hyperlink:

1. Use the **Pointer Tool** to select the object, or click for an insertion point inside the linked text. (It's not necessary to drag over a hyperlinked region of text.)

2. Click the 🖳 **Hyperlink** button on the Standard toolbar, or choose **Hyperlink...** from the Insert menu. The **Hyperlinks** dialog opens with the current link target shown. If the link is in text, the whole text link highlights.

- To modify the hyperlink, select a new link destination type and/or target.

- To remove the hyperlink, click the **Remove** button.

Removing a hyperlink does not remove the underlying object or text.

Viewing hyperlinks in your publication

The **Hyperlink Manager** gives you an overview of all the hyperlinks in your publication.

To display the Hyperlink Manager:

- Choose **Hyperlink Manager...** from the Tools menu.

The Hyperlink Manager dialog displays both object and text hyperlinks in your publication, listed by page number. The entries are in "from/to" format, showing each link's source object type and its destination page or URL.

To display a hyperlink for closer inspection:

- Click to select the link entry and click the **Display** button.

To remove or modify a hyperlink:

- Click to select the link entry and click the **Remove** or **Modify** button. To modify the hyperlink, select a new link destination type and/or target.

Adding hotspots

A hotspot is a transparent hyperlink region on a Web page. Usually placed on top of images, hotspots act like "buttons" that respond when clicked in a Web browser. They are especially useful if you want the visitor to be able to click on different parts of a picture (such as a graphic "menu" or map of your site).

To define a hotspot:

1. On the Insert menu, choose **Web Object**, and then click **Hotspot**.

2. Click and drag to draw a rectangular hotspot region. The **Hyperlinks** dialog opens.

3. Click to select the link destination type, and enter the specific hyperlink target—an Internet page, a page on your Web site, an email address, or local file.

4. Click **OK**.

To modify a hotspot hyperlink:

- Using the **Pointer** tool, double-click the hotspot.
  OR
  Click to select the hotspot, then click the 🔗 **Hyperlink** button on the Standard toolbar.

The **Hyperlinks** dialog opens with the current hotspot link target shown.

- To modify the hyperlink, select a new link destination type and/or target.

- To remove the hyperlink, click the **Remove** button.

Editing hotspots

You can move and resize hotspots on the page, just like other objects. A selected hotspot has both an outer bounding box and an inner outline, which serve different purposes.

To move or resize a hotspot:

- Click to select the hotspot.

- To move, drag from the centre, or from the hotspot's bounding box. To constrain the hotspot to vertical or horizontal movement, hold down the **Shift** key while dragging.

- To resize, drag on its outer (bounding box) handles.

By editing the inner outline, you can convert rectangular hotspots into freeform shapes that closely match the parts of the underlying graphic you want to be "hot." To edit the outline, first move the mouse pointer over the hotspot's inner outline until the cursor changes to indicate whether you're over a node or a line.

Choosing Web site colours

A Web site may have an adopted colour scheme, selected by using the **Schemes** tab. Each scheme has a name and consists of five complementary basic colours which you can apply to any design element (see **Using colour schemes** on p. 180). A selection of schemes (named "WWW 1" through "WWW 9") are specifically designed for Web use.

Web colours

Web publications have several special **Web colour** settings, usually defined as part of a colour scheme in the **Scheme Manager**. You'll need to know about these settings, even if you haven't applied scheme colours to other elements in your publication:

- The **Hyperlink** colour applies to hyperlinked text before it's been clicked on, while the same text after a visitor has clicked to "follow" the link takes on the **Followed Hyperlink** colour.

- A Web site's **Background** is a solid colour with the option of overlaying a tiled (repeated) picture, usually a bitmap pattern. The tiled picture option works just like desktop "wallpaper," so a small bitmap can go a long way. The colour scheme sample shows 🖼️ if the scheme uses a tiled bitmap. If you use a picture background with transparent regions, the Background colour is still active and will show through; otherwise the picture will cover the background colour.

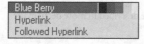

In Web Publishing mode, colour scheme samples in the Schemes tab show the Web colours along with the five basic scheme colours, as shown at left.

The easiest way to apply new Web colours is to select a different colour scheme by clicking a sample on the **Schemes** tab. You can also change any of the Web colours within a scheme using the Scheme Manager, in the same way that you would modify the scheme's five basic colours. See **Using Colour Schemes**.

Setting custom page backgrounds

The Web colours defined in the Scheme Manager normally apply throughout the site, but you can override the Scheme Manager's Background picture/colour setting for any particular page.

To set a custom page background:

1. Choose **Web Site Properties...** from the File menu.

2. On the **Background** tab, uncheck **Use Scheme Manager settings** and set new options for **Page colour** and/or **Use picture**.

> 📝 The settings apply only to the current page.

Setting Web picture display options

When you export a publication as a Web site, PagePlus applies certain global settings to determine how each image—whether drawn, pasted in, or imported—ends up as a separate bitmap displayed on the Web page.

The following conversion settings are used for Web publishing:

- Each image in the publication is exported as a separate file.

- Any image you inserted as a GIF or JPEG is exported as the original file, using its original file name.

- Inserted PNG images, metafiles, and all other graphics are converted to JPEG images, using a compression quality setting of 10 (low compression, high detail). For these images, PagePlus automatically generates file names, using incremental numbering (IMG1, IMG2, etc.) that continues each time you export.

Global export options and setting export formats are described in more detail in the PagePlus Help.

Choosing Web page properties

There's more to creating a successful Web site than designing the pages. It's a good idea to browse the **Site Properties** dialog, accessible from **File>Web Site Properties** and review a variety of settings you might not otherwise have considered!

Site Properties/Page tab

Some of the options on the dialog's **Page** tab pertain just to the current page, while others apply to the site as a whole. The Web page **title**, which will appear in the title bar of the visitor's Web browser, can serve to unify the pages and focus the site's identity, as well as aid navigation. Each page in your site can have its own title, but you may prefer to use the same title on multiple pages (in effect, a site title). An easy way to do this is to start with a blank page, give it a title, then replicate that page. Copies of that page will have the same title.

Each page also has a **file name** when it's published. You can specify file names individually; otherwise PagePlus automatically generates them. Check the instructions from your Internet Service Provider (ISP) as to their naming conventions for Home Pages and file extensions. By default, PagePlus names your first (Home) page INDEX.HTML—the standard file name a browser will be looking for. Depending on the particular server in use, however, some other name may be required. Likewise, the extension .HTM is sometimes used for pages.

Adding animation effects

PagePlus lets you add two varieties of eye-catching animation effects to any Web page: **animated marquees** and **GIF animations**. Either way, you can preview the animation and/or customize the effect. Once placed into your Web publication, the animations appear static, but they will spring to life once the site has been exported and a visitor views your page in a Web browser.

Adding sound and video

PagePlus lets you augment your Web pages with sound and video files in a variety of standard formats, including both **non-streaming** and **streaming** media. (Non-streaming files must download in entirety to a user's computer before they begin playing; streaming files require a special player that buffers incoming data and can start playing before the whole clip has arrived.)

Please see PagePlus Help for more information.

Adding Java applets

Java is a cross-platform, object-oriented programming language used to create mini-applications called **applets** that can be attached to Web pages and that run when the page is viewed in a Web browser. PagePlus lets you add Java applets to your Web publications. You don't have to write your own! Plenty of applets are available online— for example animation, interface components, live information updating, two-way interaction, and many more.

Consult PagePlus help to find out more about adding Java applets to your web pages.

Publishing a Web site to a local folder

Even though you may have saved your Web site as a PagePlus publication, it's not truly a "Web site" until you've converted it to HTML files and image files in a form that can be viewed in a Web browser. In PagePlus, this conversion process is called publishing the site. You can publish the site either to a local folder (on a hard disk) or to the Web itself. To review the basics, see **Getting started in Web mode** on p. 221.

Publishing the site to a local folder lets you preview the pages in your own browser prior to publishing them on the Web. You may find it convenient to keep your browser program open, and go back and forth between PagePlus and the browser. This way you can make changes to a single page in PagePlus, publish just the one page, then switch to your browser and preview that page to make sure everything appears just as you want it.

To publish the site to a local folder:

1. Choose **Web Site Properties...** from the File menu and double-check export settings, particularly those on the Graphics tab.

2. Choose **Publish Site** from the File menu and select **to Disk Folder...** from the submenu.

3. In the dialog, locate the folder where you wish to store the output files. If the output folder specified does not exist you'll be asked if you want a new folder created when you click **OK** to finish the dialog.

4. Either check the **Publish All Pages** option, or in the site structure tree, check which specific page(s) to publish. This can save a lot of time by skipping the export of pages you haven't changed.

5. Click **OK**.

Previewing your Web site in a browser

Previewing your site in a Web browser is an essential step before publishing it to the World Wide Web. It's the only way you can see just how your PagePlus publication will appear to a visitor. Bear in mind that pages generally load much more quickly from a hard disk than they will over the Web. If performance is sluggish from a hard disk, it's time to subtract some graphics, divide the content into more (and smaller) pages, or run the Layout Checker again.

To preview your Web site from a local hard disk:

- Choose **Publish Site** from the File menu and select **to Disk Folder...** from the submenu. After publishing the site (or selected pages), answer **Yes** when asked if you want to run a Web browser to preview your pages.
  OR

- Choose **Preview Web Site in Browser...** from the File menu. Use the dialog to specify the page range by checking/unchecking pages. Click **OK** and the publication is exported to a temporary folder.
  OR

- (if you've previously published the site to a folder) Open your Web browser and use its Open File command to display a page from the site, usually the INDEX.HTML (Home Page) file.

Publishing to the World Wide Web

Publishing to the World Wide Web involves a few more steps, but is basically as simple as publishing to a local folder! You can specify that all Web pages are published or only pages updated since your last "publish."

To publish your site to the World Wide Web:

1. On the File menu, choose **Web Site Properties...** and verify your export settings, particularly those on the **Graphics** tab.

2. On the File menu, choose **Publish Site** and then select **to Web...**.

If this is your first time publishing to the Web, the **Account Details** dialog opens (with no account information present). You'll need to set up at least one account before you can proceed.

1. In the dialog, enter the following:

- The **Account name** can be any name of your choice. You'll use it to identify this account in PagePlus (in case you have more than one).

- The **FTP address** of your Web host will be a specific URL as supplied by your Internet service provider (ISP).

- Unless directed by your provider, leave the **Port number** set at "21."

- Leave the **Folder** box blank unless directed by your provider, or if you want to publish to a specific subfolder of your root directory.

- You'll also need a **Username** and **Password**. These are pre-assigned by your provider and will most likely correspond to email login settings. Enter the password exactly as given to you, using correct upper- and lower-case spelling, or the host server may not recognize it. If you don't want to re-enter your password with each upload, check **Save password** to record the password on your computer.

- **Passive mode**: Leave checked unless you have FTP connection problems (check with your ISP). ISPs can operate passive or active FTP modes of operation.

- **Web site URL**: Set your site's URL. This allows you to view your site from a dialog after any FTP upload.

- Click **OK** to close the **Account Details** dialog.

You can also use the dialog to **Add** another account, and **Copy**, **Edit**, or **Delete** an account selected from the drop-down menu. It's a good idea to test your new or modified account by clicking the **Test** button—if the account details are valid, a dialog indicating successful connection displays.

2. If you've set up at least one account, the **Manage FTP Accounts** opens. Click the **Upload...** button to open the **Publish to Web** dialog.

    In the dialog, the last used account name is shown in the drop-down menu; its settings are displayed in subsequent boxes. You can use the drop-down menu to switch to another account, if you have set up more than one.

3. Choose which pages you want to upload—check specific page(s) in the window or **Publish All Pages**. Use the **Toggle Select**, **Toggle Branch**, and **Select All** buttons to aid page selection.

4. To safeguard your PagePlus project by upload, check the **Backup the document to the remote server** option. If the project is unsaved you'll be prompted to save it.

5. Click **OK**. PagePlus seeks an Internet connection, then:

- If uploading for the first time, selected files will be uploaded directly.
  OR

- If uploading to an existing site, an **Uploading Files** dialog is displayed showing local file action file action (whether files will be added (Add), will replace the live files (Replace), or will not be updated (Leave).

  In the dialog, select either the **Incremental Update** or **Full upload** button. Choose the former to upload only files that have altered since the last upload. You'll see a message when all files have been successfully copied. Click **OK**.

6. You'll be able to see your page(s) "live" on the Web following upload. Use the displayed **Web Site Publishing** dialog to view the site in your Web browser to the URL of your live site.

Gathering server information

If you have an email account, your contract with the email service provider may allow you a certain amount of file space (e.g., 25MB) on their server where you can store files, including the files that comprise a Web site. Or you may have a separate "Web space" arrangement with a specialized ISP. It's up to you to establish an account you can use for Web publishing.

Maintaining your Web site

Once you've **published your site** to the Web, you'll need to maintain the pages on your site by updating content periodically: adding or changing text, pictures, and links, also file/folder deletion or renaming. Making the content changes is easy enough—all the originals are right there in your publication!

To maintain files and folders on your Web site:

1. Choose **Publish Site** from the File menu and select **Maintain Web Site...** from the submenu. The Account Details dialog appears.

2. Select your FTP account name (from the drop-down menu), your Username and Password. Type the correct path in the Folder box, if required by your provider.

3. Click **Maintain**.

PagePlus seeks an Internet connection and displays a dialog showing the navigable web site's folders in a left-hand window and any selected folder's contents in the adjacent window.

4. Use standard Windows Explorer conventions to perform maintenance tasks:
   • Click on the column headers to change the current sort, or drag to change the column width.
   • The top row of buttons lets you view up one level, create a new folder, delete a selected item, upload/download a file, and refresh the window.
   • Right-click to **Open**, **Download**, **Delete**, or **Rename** any file or folder.
   • You can **Ctrl**-click to select multiple files or **Shift**-click to select a range of files.
   • To move one or more selected files, drag them into the destination folder.
   • To delete the entire web site, click the **View** button next to your selected Serif Manifest file—in the dialog, click the **Delete all managed files** button.

   Remember to use the lower information window which displays a running log of each maintenance task and its status.

5. When you're done, click the window's ⊠ **Close** button to terminate the FTP connection and return to PagePlus.

Index

—Z—